I kept waiting for this book
something harsh rather than
more harmful than helpful. h̲ ᴜ.ᴜ ..ᴜ. ᴜ.ᴜ . ᴜᴜ ᴜ
have a nudge to find accessible ways to get your inner world out,
Marc's step by step contribution to this adventure is for you. Read
slowly, take your time, play with the work, and thank me later!

Wm. Paul Young
Author, *The Shack, Crossroads* and *Eve.*

Marc Alan Schelske's manual on journaling is among the most
accessible and practical guides that I've encountered. As someone
prone to binges and famines in my devotional writing, his
contribution of patterns and principles that become healthy
habits is an invaluable tool. Six weeks for a new way of being? Yes
please!

Dr. Bradley Jersak
Dean of Theology & Culture, St. Stephen's University, author, *Out of
the Embers: Faith After the Great Deconstruction.*

Some books about spiritual disciplines load up heavy burdens on
the reader: ought's, should's, more, better, now... but not this one.
Marc's Journaling for Spiritual Growth invites you into an
exploration of your life, developing the habit of journaling as you
go. Simple, profound, and entirely practical, he guides the reader
into the easy gift of journaling. This resource is a treasure; I
highly recommend it.

Matt Tebbe
Co-founder Gravity leadership, co-pastor, The Table, co-author,
Having the Mind of Christ: Eight Axioms to Cultivate a Robust Faith.

Marc has a deep awareness that there are significant things
happening in and around us, ours to discover if we only pay
attention. This book is a friend for the journey, walking with us to
discover the craft of journaling with curiosity and a sense of
adventure.

Mandy Smith
Pastor and author, *Unfettered: Imagining a Childlike Faith Beyond the
Baggage of Western Culture* and *The Vulnerable Pastor.*

Highly practical and research-driven yet rooted in the mystical tradition, Journaling for Spiritual Growth is an accessible, gentle guide to exploring your spiritual life. Written for everyone from the merely curious to the deeply religious, you will find tools, training, and companionship for your journey. Perfect for groups or solo use, this will be of great benefit to anyone looking to cultivate greater awareness of God's presence in their life.

Jonathan Puddle
Pastor and author, *You are Enough: Learning to Love Yourself the Way God Loves You* and *Mornings With God: Daily Bible Devotional for Men.*

Journaling for Spiritual Growth invites you to a reflective and meditative life of spiritual growth and health. This gentle, step-by-step guide makes the abstract practical and doable. If journaling feels intimidating to you, or if you've tried and failed to develop this practice in the past, this grace-filled guide removes the stumbling blocks, equipping and encouraging you in a sustainable life of journaling. Wherever you are on your spiritual journey, you'll find space with Marc to bring your life before God through reflective listening and learning. As you grow in the practice of being present to God and yourself, you'll find the transformation and renewal you seek.

Susan Carson
Director, Roots&Branches Network, Author, *Rooted (IN): Thriving in Connection with God, Yourself, and Others.*

JOURNALING FOR SPIRITUAL GROWTH

MARC ALAN SCHELSKE

SIX WEEKS TO BUILD A HABIT THAT FOSTERS SPIRITUAL AND EMOTIONAL MATURITY

Editor: Leanne Sype
Mental Health Consultant: Cindy Brosh
Cover Design & Interior Art: Tamara Zabaznoska
Interior Design: 2:ten Creative

2nd Edition, Expanded and Updated.
Print ISBN 978-0-9886882-2-3
Digital ISBN 978-0-9886882-3-0

Published in the United States by
Live210 Media
PO Box 220213
Portland, Oregon 97269

To Emerson

and so many others who, like me,

must learn how to live well with a chronically

curious, fragmented, and busy mind.

ACKNOWLEDGEMENTS

I am indebted to Christina, Emerson, and Lucas who give me space to write and cheer me on; my church family at Bridge City who encourage and help me work through all my ideas; and the many who interact kindly with me on the internet. I hope my words can be of use in your journey of spiritual growth.

Much thanks to the hospitality the kind Benedictine monks of Mount Angel Abbey, in Mount Angel, Oregon, where much of this book was written.

My deep gratitude goes out to my brave and generous beta readers. This book is better because of you: Janine Smith, Raymon Yates, Tracy English, Kim Bruce, Kim Puckett, Michael Martin, Sylvia Harrison, and Bernhard Gildemeister. I'm especially indebted to Raynna Myers and Anne Lafleur who went above and beyond with in-depth feedback and insight.

I am so thankful for the many folks who helped bring this book to life: Cindy Brosh, who made sure my references to the brain and matters pertaining to mental health were both accurate and helpful; Leanne Sype, who is not only a skilled and gracious editor, but helped make my words more sensitive; Jonathan Puddle, who shared much wise counsel on the book and the publishing process; Susan Carson, who made launching the book fun and effective. I'll never do this process alone again!

Thanks as well to the folks who made the amazing writing software Ulysses. This project was so much easier for your work. Finally, I want to acknowledge K.J. Ramsey and her designer, Conrad Garner, for the cover of her book, *The Lord is My Courage*, which so moved me and served as inspiration for the incredible artwork that graces the cover of this book.

CONTENTS

INTRODUCTION

OR HOW TO USE THIS BOOK

This is not a book for reading, not really. It's a book to guide you in *doing*. You certainly can read it right through, but there is a better way. Let me tell you a bit of what this book is about, and how I might be able to help you through these pages.

I'm going to assume that you've picked this up because you believe there is such a thing as spiritual growth.* I expect you desire a healthier inner life and more profound experience of God. You believe or hope this is possible. I've spent more than twenty-five years helping people with these very things. It's not uncommon for me to find myself sitting on my front deck or at a coffee shop in a conversation with someone like you about the inner life.

What I share in this little book has been tested over more than two decades, shaped by personal experience, and sharpened as I've worked with others. There are many spiritual practices and many different personalities. What works for one won't always work for another. Yet, I stand convinced that, for many, journaling is an effective and transformative spiritual practice. This book, however, is not about convincing you.

I start with this assumption: You are here to try something new or you want to strengthen an existing journaling practice. That's why reading this book isn't sufficient. Journaling is a practice you learn by doing. Reading is a frontal lobe activity, where your brain assembles the puzzle of letters, words, and grammar in order to synthesize ideas. Cataloging new ideas isn't the same thing as spiritual growth, though. Spiritual growth happens in our inner world. It runs deep into our limbic system

---

* Spiritual growth? What does that even mean!? Glad you asked. This word means a thousand different things to different people. In short, I use "spiritual" to refer to the essence of who we are, and "spiritual growth" to refer to both the process and steps we take to nurture our growth as human beings. If you'd like more clarity on where I'm coming from, and the connection between spirituality and religion, you'll find a short essay on spiritual growth in Appendix 1.

touching parts of us that are older than words.* This is the domain of Spirit. It is, if I can use a controversial term, mystical. We are entering the world of experience.

Of course, you'll be reading. This is a book after all, but your reading must serve the more important goal of experience. You and I are going to try something books are ill-suited to accomplish. First, we're going to help you build a new habit. Second, while that's happening, I hope to help you have an experience that goes deeper than your intellect. My part is to share my experience organized into a path you can follow. Your part—and this is key—is to *do the thing* and then think about what happens. Literally do the thing. Journal.

I first prepared these ideas in a simple six-week course, delivered as a series of weekly emails. People seemed to find this helpful, so I expanded those emails into a short ebook. Almost a thousand people used this material in those original forms. I still get requests for it. I've re-written and expanded that material to include insight about how habits are built and important lessons I've learned about journaling since those first emails.

In order to walk you through the process of building a habit, I've kept the original structure. Six weeks, five lessons each week, each with a short reading and a journaling exercise. Five lessons per week mean you can take weekends off or have a margin of time to catch up when you fall behind. The readings present key principles. The exercises help you move from information to experience, taking small steps toward building your new habit. Each week's lessons are tied together by a certain theme.

Week 1 suggests that a successful journaling practice begins not with our choice of tools or techniques, but with certain perspectives. For some, this might seem a strange place to begin. Shouldn't we start by grabbing a journal? In my experience, no. Far more important than whether you journal in a blank notebook or on a computer screen is *why* you're journaling at all.

---

* The limbic system is the complex system that includes nerves, brain structures, and "response software" that both initiates and interprets the bodily and mental experience of emotions. This includes the amygdala, the hippocampus, and the hypothalamus, which all play a role in our survival drives. In terms of consciousness, the limbic system seems to be the seat of our instincts, emotions, and moods.

Week 2 covers the tools necessary for journaling, although this extends beyond what you might think. Week 3 covers the essential elements that make journaling for spiritual growth different from other kinds of journaling. In week 4, I suggest a particular template for journaling and why using a template is one secret to a long-term, successful journaling practice. During this week, you'll experience several different templates.

By week 5, you'll be journaling. With that in mind, the theme of week 5 is habits. We'll cover how habits are built, including important lessons we can learn from our bad habits. We'll talk about what gets in the way and how we can use the principles that build strong habits in support of journaling. Week 6 brings us to the end of the journey by talking about the principles necessary to continue journaling over the long haul. At the end of the book, you'll find additional material to support you in the journey, but we'll get to all of that in time.

From the very beginning, each lesson will end with a question or two in a section called **Practice**. I encourage you to write your responses down, whether on paper or in a digital writing space, like a journaling app on your tablet or a document on your computer. Even though you won't officially be journaling until later, those early written responses are practice for the habit you are building.

If you prefer to read the book without taking it day-by-day or doing the responses, by all means do. Most should be able to read it through in less than three hours. If, however, your goal is spiritual growth, then consider these pages a convenient way for us to be together briefly each day. If you take the book one day at a time actually doing the things I invite you to do, by the end of the six weeks you will be journaling. You'll be well on your way to building a sustainable, long-term habit. Depending on your reading speed and how deeply you engage the journaling prompts, you should be able to move through this process spending 20-30 minutes a day. Some days are a bit shorter, others a bit longer. (And certainly, if you want to go deep, your responses can take as long as you like!)

You may have already noticed that I use footnotes. I use them so that I can keep the text flowing smoothly while including asides, commentary, clarification of terms, and a few references. Read them or not, as you like.

Oh, one more thing. I am a Christian pastor. While I read broadly and learn from many teachers, spiritual formation following the way of Jesus is both what I teach and what has primarily shaped my own spiritual story. My faith community considers the Bible our central resource for spiritual growth.* In this book, I will reference passages from the Bible and refer to God using language and metaphors from my faith tradition. I attempted to do so in a way that would be hospitable and helpful to people from any background. Yet I must acknowledge that there are many who have had painful experiences associated with Christians, pastors, or the Bible. If you are among them, I'm so sorry. I don't want these words of mine to injure you further. If the best path forward for you is to set this book aside, please return it to where you bought it, or if that's not possible, get in touch with me at Marc@MarcAlanSchelske.com, and I will gladly refund your purchase price.

Having said that, a wide variety of people from different backgrounds and faith traditions have found this process safe and helpful. If you don't identify as Christian or don't find scripture helpful for your spiritual growth, you can adapt the language to suit your needs. I know from long-tested experience that this method of interior reflection results in growth. I believe the Spirit will meet you where you are and guide your growth regardless of the words you use, so long as your posture is open. (And that's true for anyone from any faith, including my own.)

That's my counsel for you on how best to use this book. I am envisioning sitting with you on my front deck. You've told me you want your life to be different, deeper. I can sense you're serious, so I ask if I can share something that's worked for me and many others. I ask if you're really willing to give it a try. You nod your head, and we begin.

---

*The Bible is well known as the book of Christian scripture, but it's more accurate to understand it not as a book but as a library of books assembled over time. That library includes the ancient Jewish scriptures written in Hebrew, known as the *Tanakh*, as well as a smaller number of books written in Greek by some of the earliest followers of Jesus.

CHOOSE THE RIGHT PERSPECTIVE

Journaling is not a secret technique. Therapists, spiritual directors, pastors, and coaches recommend it. There are diet journals and gratitude journals, bullet journals and dream journals. We hold the journals of historical figures like Lewis & Clark or Anne Frank in high regard.

Journaling is time-tested. In my experience personally and with others, journaling is the spiritual practice that most consistently results in real growth. This claim, however, does not apply to most of what passes for journaling. We're not talking about keeping a diary, writing a memoir, or tracking habits like diet or water intake. Those have their place, but this is not that.

Journaling for spiritual growth is a very particular kind of journaling practice. This first week we'll explore how this practice is different from other things we might imagine when we think of journaling.

THERE IS NO SHORTCUT

READ & REFLECT

Microwaves. Next-day delivery. On-demand video streaming. We are an impatient culture. We want what we want when we want it. Instant convenience affirms our sense of control. We're wise to be so efficient! We network instead of building relationships. Instead of reading, we skim. We only listen halfway because we're already formulating a response. We congratulate ourselves on our hustle, then wonder why we feel so frazzled.

Reality stubbornly ignores our impatience. There is no shortcut to what matters. Good crusty bread takes time. An inspiring Olympic performance took tedious practice. There's no fresh produce without a gardener who tended the soil through the long growing season.

Spiritual growth is more garden than restaurant. God gives the growth, but doesn't barge in forcing us to be better people. We are invited to cultivate the soil of our hearts so we can receive the growth God offers. Like a well-tended garden, a faithful journaling practice bears fruit. This isn't because journaling is magic. What matters is not the book, the pen, or even the words. What makes journaling work is the shape of the practice. The task of writing words focuses our attention, slows our pace, and encourages reflection.

According to Plato, one of Socrates' last lines was that the unexamined life is not worth living.* John Dewey, an educator and philosopher, said we don't learn through experience alone but by reflecting on our experiences.† Augustine prayed: "God…

---

* Plato. Apology 38a. *Plato in Twelve Volumes*, Vol. 1. Cambridge, MA, Harvard University Press; London 1966.

† This is not a direct quote from Dewey, but a summary of his premise, most clearly articulated in the chapter called "Experience and Thinking," in his book *Democracy and Education*.

let me know myself, let me know You."* The call to examine our own hearts echoes throughout scripture.

One example is Lamentations 3:40: "Let us test and examine our ways."† When we take time to reflect on what is happening to us and within us, on how we responded and why, we begin to notice patterns. Spiritual growth happens slowly and through intentional reflection. In the same way, forming a new habit takes time. Neuroscience has shown that repetition over time forms new neural pathways. That's why we're walking through the process together, one day at a time, over six weeks. For both spiritual growth and building a journaling practice, there isn't a shortcut.

PRACTICE

Each day the **Read & Reflect** section will be followed by an opportunity to **Practice**. These exercises are not frosting on the cake; they are the cake. I've designed each to help you do two things. First, the exercise will get you thinking about the big idea from the reading. Second, it will provide a tangible step toward building a habit of journaling. Plan on spending 15 minutes, more or less, on these prompts. If you have the time and desire to go deeper, please do.

I know that writing down responses as a part of these exercises sounds a lot like journaling, but you're not officially starting to journal yet. I say that because some people invest the idea of journaling with a great deal of weight. They want to do it

---

* Augustine, *Soliloquies*, Book II 2.1.1.

† Lamentations 3:40, NRSV. Need an orientation? This is a reference to a specific passage in the Bible. The reference (Lamentations 3:40) is an address. Lamentations is the the book. 3:40 refers to the chapter (ch. 3) and verse (v. 40). With this address you can find this verse in any version of the Bible. Of course, to do this you'll need a Bible. If you don't have one on hand, there are many free online options. *BibleGateway.com* is one. If you don't have a preference, I recommend using either the New International Version (NIV) or the New Revised Standard Version. (NRSV). The NIV is a bit easier to read, and is the most commonly used English translation. The NRSV is a bit clunkier sounding, but a bit more literally translated. If you're new to this whole thing and wonder why the heck there are versions for something like the Bible (I mean, didn't God write it?!) you can learn more about that in a 3-part blog series I wrote: *https://marcalanschelske.com/good-bible-1/*

just right. They want to get the perfect blank book and a good pen. If you feel that kind of anxiety coming up in you, take a deep breath. You and I are going to walk slowly, step-by-step, toward that goal. Just take each day as it comes, one step at a time, and trust that some of the things you're here to learn, you will only learn by doing.

Here's today's exercise:

◆ **Journal on your relationship to rushing.**

You can use any or all of these prompts:

- **Where in your life do you tend to rush?**
- **Why do you rush in these areas?**
- **How does rushing serve you?**
- **What might you be missing out on by rushing?**

Oh, before you start, **a few quick instructions.**

When I say "Journal on" the day's question, I mean that you should write out your answer, giving time and attention to truthful reflection on your own experience. You're here to start a habit of journaling. You're going to be writing a little each day. I hope that's not surprising.

At this point—this is really important—don't get bogged down on the question of format (pen and paper? A Word document? A journaling app?) We'll attend to all of that later. For today, pick a format that's immediately accessible, and give yourself 15 minutes to slowly think through the questions posed. During the second week we'll consider the different tools carefully; meanwhile, use whatever is most convenient.

Don't just think your answers. Thoughts are notoriously mushy. It is deceptively hard for the same brain having a thought to reflect on the thought it's having. Writing forces us to crystalize thoughts into words. This slows our minds and shifts us into meta-cognition, that necessary thinking-about-thinking that is the seedbed of all personal awareness and deep insight.

Also, don't try to *be a writer*. This isn't about creativity or grammar or beautiful prose. The words are just a handle. You can bullet-point your thoughts. You can use incomplete sentences. Nobody's grading this. Your goal is clarity. When you read the words back, are they true? Are they fair? Do they capture your thoughts? If not, change them.

OK, now you know enough to get started.

NEITHER DIARY, NOR ARTWORK

READ & REFLECT

Imagine someone journaling. What image springs to mind? A writer laboring over each word in their black notebook? A teenager crying into a diary, recording their roller-coaster of love and emotion? An artist with a fistful of colored pens, working in their bullet journal or sketchbook? None of these images are helpful. Before we go into the specifics of journaling for spiritual growth, it may help to clear away some unhelpful assumptions.

A journal is not a diary.

Journaling for spiritual growth is not keeping a record of what happened each day. Journaling will touch on the events of your life, but those details are not the point. Your goal is to reflect on who you are and who you are becoming. Banish the thought that you'll be recording every event, thought, or feeling.

A journal is not an heirloom.

Some visualize a handcrafted leather cover enfolding artisanal paper, elegant handwriting spanning the pages. It might occur to you that years from now a collection of your reflections would be a treasure for your kids. It's embarrassing to admit that in my early journaling experiences, I fell headlong for this trap. I started imagining the people who, one day, would discover and read my words, and I subtly shifted to writing for an audience. When you're writing for other people, though, an invisible editor slips between your thoughts and the page. Instead of being truthful, you begin to curate. Journaling for spiritual growth is a private practice. It may be helpful to think of it as a form of prayer. It's not meant for others. The contents of your heart and mind are not always presentable, orderly, or even coherent! Your journal doesn't need to be either.

A journal is not creative writing.

Another common misconception is that journaling is a creative practice, a mobile workshop for the budding lyricist or novelist. This undermines the purpose of journaling, and even pushes it out of reach for those who don't think themselves creative. Our intention here is not to practice writing or make art. We are seeking spiritual growth through the process of externalizing and reflecting on certain thoughts, feelings, and experiences in conversation with God. The journaling process can and should be raw and unedited.

A journal is not a Bible study.

Because we're pursuing journaling as a spiritual practice, some Christians imagine it must be a form of Bible study. Keeping a journal or log of insight from scripture is a worthwhile practice, but it's not what we're doing here. Scripture certainly can be part of this kind of journaling practice. It often is for me, but we must stay clear on our purpose. Our journaling time is not the venue for learning Bible knowledge or gathering support for certain doctrines. Soon I'll give you some examples of how you might include scripture in ways that support spiritual growth.

A journal is not a mountain top experience

There's one last obstacle I should warn you away from. People who are just starting out in the pursuit of deeper spirituality often do so because they've had some kind of "mountain top" experience. That's a phrase from my religious background that refers to the spiritual high you might get at a particularly good retreat. You felt God's nearness. Maybe it seemed life-changing. It's not uncommon to want to chase that euphoric feeling. Journaling cannot bear up under this expectation. Journaling is a day-in-day-out kind of practice. I've had a few mystical experiences while journaling, but most days it feels exactly like reading some things and writing some things. Not at all very special.

Misconceptions like these will impede a sustainable habit of journaling. Try to document every event and feeling and you'll get bogged down. Fuss over every word and journaling won't be sustainable. Start writing for an audience and your journal will become a form of image-crafting, the very opposite of spiritual growth. Even Bible study can become an obstacle for growth when used to bypass the real issues of your heart.*

The process of journaling for spiritual growth helps you externalize and understand your inner life. As such, it is not for anyone beyond you and the Spirit. We'll soon talk more about how to go about this, but for today, spend some time reflecting on your preconceptions and how they might get in your way.

PRACTICE

◆ **Journal on your preconceptions about journaling.**

Use any or all of these prompts:

- **What images come to mind when you hear the word** *journal*?

- **What kinds of people do you imagine journal regularly? Why?**

- **What past experiences have you had with journaling? How were those experiences helpful or unhelpful?**

- **If you journaled in the past but didn't continue, why do you think you stopped?**

Keep this in mind: There is no right answer. The goal is to inventory your previous experiences and preconceptions and then reflect on how they've impacted your ideas about journaling.

---

* A psychotherapist named John Welwood coined the useful term, "spiritual bypassing." He was describing how some religious people use scripture, prayer, and dogmatic faith statements as a way to avoid facing the discomfort of painful emotions and circumstances. Spiritual bypassing can be a helpful coping tool in the midst of an overwhelming experience, but when particular practices or doctrine keep you from being honest about your hurts, those things impede healing and growth.

IT'S A MIRROR

READ & REFLECT

You have no first-hand experience of what your face looks like. Others do. They have an unmediated view you just can't see. In order to see your own face, you need an external tool that temporarily relocates your observer self. I know that's a weird way to describe a mirror or camera, but it's also accurate. Without these external tools it's simply not possible to see your own face.

That external perspective is a gift. How else would we know we have spinach in our teeth? The mirror or camera enables you to see what you otherwise could not. That's the essence of journaling for spiritual growth; the process holds up a mirror allowing you to see into your inner life.

Our interior experience is a muddle of swirling senses, feelings, drives, thoughts, and spiritual movement. Our thinking brain, the cerebral cortex, curates this raw material into a conscious presentation of "what we're seeing" or "what we're thinking." It feels objective, only it's not. It's a constructed point of view that prioritizes some things and leaves others out.* Journaling enables us to order that muddle using particular words. Because our intention is spiritual growth, I'll invite you to reflect on those words in light of God's presence and guidance.† Doing so opens a window into your inner life.

In my journaling, I've often caught helpful glimpses into who I really am and why. I've noticed recurring motivations. I've clarified tangled emotions and learned what the ache in my gut signifies. I've connected dots that helped me understand how my

---

* An example of this mental curation is the Baader–Meinhof phenomenon. Once I was shopping for a particular model car. Shortly, I began to notice that exact model everywhere. Did they suddenly manifest? No. They had always been there, part of the constant background data of perception. When that object mattered to me, my mind curated my attention so I was able to see what had always been there. This quirk is also called the Frequency Illusion.

† Not comfortable with God language? That's fine. Substitute language that works for you. More on this soon.

past is still shaping my present. Through journaling, you may discover layers of insecurity. You may find yourself able to name feelings that used to be confusing fog. You might see behind the armor of anger to the tender hurts and fears beneath. You may notice patterns of self-protection that limit your capacity to love. It's not only hard things that surface, though. I've also seen the glimmering light of Spirit's presence in moments of beauty, belonging, and reconciliation. You'll see that, too.

Journaling is nearly an ideal tool to see into ourselves for personal and spiritual growth. You can't take the spinach out of your teeth if you don't know it's there.

PRACTICE

◆ **Reflect on a situation where someone else saw something true about you that you hadn't seen yourself.**

Start with any or all of these prompts:

- **Briefly recall the situation. Who saw you more clearly than you saw yourself? What did they see?**

- **What was it like to be told something about yourself that you didn't know?**

- **How did this experience impact your life going forward?**

WEEK 1, DAY 4
YOUR PERSONAL GROWTH ASSISTANT

READ & REFLECT

You want to mature personally and spiritually. That's a daunting task! Fortunately, you are accompanied by a helpful personal assistant. This assistant wants you to flourish. Their only concern is your safety. Sounds useful, right? The trouble is that communication with this assistant can be tricky. In some cases, they scream. Other times, they barely whisper. To make matters worse, you've very likely been trained to ignore them or to misinterpret their messages. Who is this personal assistant that's always present, works ceaselessly for your safety, and can be so hard to understand?

Your emotions. All your experience—every sensation, new idea, relationship, and conversation—has been filtered through your limbic system. The limbic system is the complex network of nerves, brain structures, and "response software" that both initiates and interprets the bodily and mental experience of emotions.[*]

Many of us were taught that emotions are the transient side-effect of experience, which means they are a distraction from clear-headed logic. We elevate reason as more mature, even more spiritual, while we denigrate emotion as flighty, subjective, and immature. This is unhelpful mythology from a pre-scientific world.

Your brain is wired in such a way that it is just not possible to have an experience without the associated sensory input passing

---

[*] It comes as a surprise to many that emotions are primarily bodily experiences, but this is what the best current science indicates. In very simple terms, the body adopts certain postures in reaction to both inner and outer triggers—certain muscles tense, blood flow increases or decreases, heart rate changes, the eyes focus or squint. The limbic system constantly scans the body and reports this information in terms of mental sensations that we call emotions. This is part of why body language is so important to us, and why those of us who have become disconnected from a sense of our body have such a hard time with relationships. The body and emotions are intimately connected.

through and being interpreted by the limbic system.* The bodily and mental experience of emotion is an integrated part of how your brain structures sensory information and gives that data meaning.

What does this mean for personal, emotional, and spiritual growth? Becoming aware of our emotions and learning how to wisely understand them are essential skills for maturity. Growing spiritually does not mean becoming less emotional. Instead, as we mature we become more capable of holding and understanding our emotions as well as the emotions of others. We become less likely to be overwhelmed, or when we do find ourselves in an emotional flood, we recover more quickly.

Emotions will necessarily be part of your journaling practice. Perhaps you're more in tune with your emotions. Then you'll find it easy to incorporate the insight of your emotions into your journaling. Or you may be more like me. For many reasons, including temperament, childhood trauma, and religious training, I spent much of my life disconnected from my emotions. Learning to listen to them was difficult. If that's true of you, it is crucial you learn how to listen to the input your personal assistant is offering.

If you're resistant to this idea or if you're one of the many Christians who were taught that emotions are untrustworthy or even a temptation, you'll struggle with what I teach in the coming days. Ignoring the way emotions shape your inner world is a bit like choosing to walk with only one leg. If God gave you two functional legs, shouldn't you use both?

If you're uncertain about the validity of this idea or would like more understanding about how emotions work and what they mean, I invite you to take a break from this book and read *The Wisdom of Your Heart: Discovering the God-given Purpose and Power of Your Emotions*. There you'll hear about my journey of emotional growth. I address myths often taught in Christian communities about emotions with corrective insight from scripture. Finally, I present our current understanding of what

---

* Including reading the Bible and talking about theology, which has interesting implications.

happens inside our brains and bodies during the experience of emotion and how this can help us understand what they mean.[*]

Journaling for spiritual growth is not therapy. Yet, because of how your brain works, emotions unavoidably play a role in this process. This personal assistant is with you at all times. Their only goal is your safety—even when they misunderstand the world around you or when you misinterpret what they're saying. Learning to listen to what your emotions have to say is vital.

PRACTICE

◆ **Journal about your relationship with your own emotions.**

Use any of the following prompts if you need help getting started:

- **Do you think of yourself as more emotional or unemotional? Why?**

- **How has this posture shaped your life?**

- **Reflect on times when this personal assistant gave you helpful information that you either used or disregarded.**

- **Imagine a person who is emotionally self-aware and becoming spiritually mature. What do you suspect the role of emotions is in their lives? In what ways might emotion help them in their journey of spiritual growth.**

- **Now, imagine you are that person. What is the constructive role that emotions can play in your spiritual growth?**

----

[*] You can learn more about my book and find links to where you can get it here: https://marcalanschelske.com/the-wisdom-of-your-heart/

WEEK 1, DAY 5

UNDERSTAND HOW WE LEARN

READ & REFLECT

Spiritual growth can be a nebulous idea. Let's make it more concrete. In simplest terms, spiritual growth is learning. It frequently, but not always, comes at the expense of painful life experiences. This kind of learning shapes our character, not just our ideas and thoughts. In the New Testament book of Romans, the Apostle Paul calls the process of spiritual growth "the renewing of our minds."[*]

If spiritual growth is learning, then it's helpful to think about how we learn. Some of what we learn barely sticks; other lessons penetrate deeply. It may help to think of learning in terms of three different modes: Surface learning, Embedded learning, and Reflective learning.

Surface learning happens every day. We encounter a new fact, like someone's name or phone number. This information enters short-term memory. If it stands out in some way—as unique, funny, very useful, or emotionally impactful—we'll retain it longer. Otherwise, life provides an unending cascade of new information that will shortly displace that new fact. Unless we push that new information into long-term memory in some way, perhaps through repetition or other memory association tool, it will shortly disappear.

Surface learning is part of navigating the world but doesn't seem to make much impact on our character. We know this. Getting a degree in ethics doesn't create an ethical person. Memorizing scripture doesn't mean a person will be more compassionate.

Embedded learning pushes the lesson deeper. We have an experience that's emotionally charged in some way. Perhaps it's exciting, painful, or even scary. Our limbic system associates that

---

[*] "Do not be conformed to this world, but be transformed by the renewing of your minds, so that you may discern what is the will of God—what is good and acceptable and perfect." Romans 12:2, NRSV.

visceral feeling with the raw sensory data of the experience. Immediately, automatically, and often unconsciously, the mind generates a story to explain what's happening and why. The stronger the emotional anchor, and the more deeply the experience impacts our survival or sense of identity, the more deeply this story is embedded. These embedded stories shape how we see ourselves, others, and the world.*

Here's an example. When I was nine or so, I was bitten by the paperboy's dog. The dog seemed like a giant. I thought he was going to kill me. This happened more than forty years ago. I've had countless safe interactions with dogs since. Yet, whenever I hear a dog's guttural growl, I experience an echo of my childhood fear. The hair on the back of my neck stands up. Adrenaline pumps. Anxiety rises in my chest. Even when it's my dog!

That dog bite was a minor trauma. Many experience much, much worse. Do you see how embedded learning works? Negative or very painful experiences like trauma, abuse, fear, or great shame lock learning deep in our hearts. We take on a story about ourselves, other people, the world, or even our concept of God. Visceral experiences that are positive, like profound experiences of love, forgiveness, or having a divine encounter of some kind, can impact us similarly. Strong emotion is the sledgehammer that drives the learning deep into our psyche. The more powerful the emotion, the more deeply the learning is etched into our hearts and minds. Unlike surface learning, embedded learning shapes our character and automatic responses, even when we don't want it to!

Surface learning and embedded learning are not generally under our control, but personal, emotional, and spiritual growth requires active and intentional participation. Here we use the third kind of learning. This one we can initiate. Reflective learning happens when we focus on some aspect of our experience and purposefully reflect on it. We look for connections. We pay attention to the emotions that accompanied

---

* Traumatic memory is a particularly powerful example of this mental process. Because of the way memories are stored, when a current situation echoes an earlier unresolved trauma, all the feelings and body states from the original incident flood back in. For someone who is not prepared or who doesn't understand this, those flooding feelings are often experienced as coming from the current situation.

the experience in the past as well as the current emotions we have about that past event. We think about how we reacted and why, beginning to notice patterns, context, and meaning. Consciously engaging our thoughts and feelings is the secret sauce for personal, emotional, and spiritual growth. This is what makes most modes of recovery work and therapy effective. When we do this kind of reflective learning with a prayerful mindset, it becomes the gateway to spiritual maturity.

There are several reasons why reflective learning is necessary for growth. It slows our natural tendency toward fast-paced unreflective living. Our normal hurried pace lets us gloss over our inner experience, skating around problems on the thin ice of denial. We leap to conclusions that reinforce the most convenient (often most self-justifying) story. Facing the truth about our inner lives is frequently difficult, sometimes even painful. Naturally we avoid this kind of discomfort, but in doing so we also avoid growth. A rushed mind has little time to know itself and rarely senses God.

Reflective learning also allows us to see ourselves. If you run past a mirror, you may catch your reflection out of the corner of your eye, but you won't see yourself accurately. The slow pace of reflective learning creates space for us to look at ourselves truthfully.

Finally, reflective learning teaches inner listening. Growing up in a Christian family, I was taught to pray. By this, I mean that I was taught to present my needs and wants to God. Maybe you had a similar experience. With this background, it's easy to reduce prayer to a spiritual grocery list. Few of us were taught to sit still and listen for God's voice in our interior. That's much harder.

In the Gospel of John, Jesus makes a promise that God's Spirit would be available to teach us.[*] Yet scripture also suggests

---

[*] "But the Advocate, the Holy Spirit, whom the Father will send in my name, will teach you everything, and remind you of all that I have said to you." John 14:26, NRSV.

that the Spirit most often speaks in a "still, small voice."* That's why Psalms 46 tells us that to know God, we must "be still."† Our spiritual ears are not attuned to noise.

Journaling isn't a diary, or creative writing, or a collection of deep thoughts. It's so much more. Your journal is a sanctuary where you bring your life before God through reflective listening and learning.

PRACTICE

◆ **Journal on how Surface, Embedded and Reflective learning have shown up in your life.**

Use any of these prompts:

- **Where have you experienced these three kinds of learning in your life? How have they shaped you?**

- **How have these modes of learning been part of your spiritual or religious journey? Which has made the most difference for you? Why do you think that is?**

- **If reflective learning were an intentional and regular part of your life, how do you imagine your life would be different?**

---

* In 1st Kings 19, we find an ancient story of a prophet hearing God's voice. He has several dramatic experiences, and though he expects God to speak in those impressive ways, that is not where he hears God's voice. Finally, he is able to hear God speaking in silence. The phrase "still, small voice," comes to us from an old English translation of 1 Kings 19:12. Other translations include "the sound of silence," "a whispered hush," or even "a quiet wind."

† "Be still and know that I am God." Psalms 46:10, many versions.

PREPARE YOUR TOOLS

A practice of journaling for spiritual growth need not be mysterious or complicated. The process can easily adapt to your needs and season of life. Even so, some essential tools are necessary.

When I mention tools, you likely picture notebooks, pens, or a blank document on a screen. Those are certainly necessary and we'll talk about them soon. It may surprise you, however, that the tangible implements you journal with are the least important tools in your toolbox.

Journaling won't happen by accident. Cramming it inconsistently into the corners of your life won't work. You're here to build a habit, which requires frequency and consistency. To help your new habit take root we need to lower the threshold of difficulty. Additionally, this is journaling *for* spiritual growth. We're not journaling for its own sake; we're doing this to grow. You'll be looking into your inner world, bringing yourself before God to practice reflection.

This week we'll talk about the tools necessary to nurture these intentions. Over time, you'll adapt the practice so it works well for your personality and life, but as long as you stick with these essentials, you'll stay on track.

Gracious Flexibility

Read & Reflect

Trees surround my home. We've got twelve-foot arborvitae on two sides of our yard. A massive spreading Japanese maple occupies the center with various ornamental trees around the edges. Towering over our neighborhood are a dozen or so giant evergreens of various kinds.

One recent winter our trees were put to the test. First, we had a massive windstorm. Branches whipped. The giant evergreens swayed precariously. Some branches couldn't hold on. After a few hours, our yard was filled with debris. About two months later we had a record-breaking ice storm. Ice, almost a half-inch thick, encased everything. The thin branches of the Japanese maple formed a matrix of ice. Our shrubs were solid blocks. High above, the evergreen branches drooped and creaked under hundreds of pounds of ice.

Then came the melt. Ice, water, and branches fell continuously for hours. Branches that had barely survived the wind couldn't bear up under the ice. The cracks of breaking branches and thumps of falling ice sounded like we were sheltering in the middle of a battlefield. Which branches survived? In most cases, the trees that were healthy and flexible made it through. The old dry branches, the ones hollowed out by rot, the brittle ones, fell.

When it comes to building habits, most people believe the conventional wisdom: Set up a routine and stick to it religiously. Repetition builds habits, so we're told to perform the new routine in the same way, with the same tools, in the same space and time every day. That's how you build a habit, isn't it?

Life rarely conforms to our preferences. We're called to work early. The kids get sick, so we clear our schedule to care for them. Circumstances force us to react and we cannot stick with our ideal routine. Maybe we use an app or a daily check-off sheet to track our new routine. Each missed day becomes a gap in our success. At some point, those gaps weigh more heavily than the original hope of change. The result? We quit. Even worse, we may decide that this sort of habit doesn't work. At least, it doesn't work for us. I can't count how many new habits I've abandoned over the years thanks to this cycle. Habits are indeed built more quickly by faithful repetition, yet very few of us have lives that allow us to do the same thing, in the same way, at the same time, and in the same space, every day for weeks. Does that mean we are out of luck when it comes to building new habits?

Of course not! Look at your life. You already have any number of habits you keep returning to, even if you can't do them every day. If you miss a day brushing your teeth, you don't give up on the idea altogether! We start by accepting life as it is: varied, marked by the unexpected, and often out of our control. Even so, we still find ways to do what matters to us, even if we have to do them differently from time to time.

If your ideal routine is to journal in the morning, that's great —it's what I do—but some mornings don't allow for it. Sometimes my preferred tools aren't with me. I like to journal in a quiet space with a cup of tea, but I don't always get what I want. What do we do when our ideal routine isn't possible?

The first crucial tool to build a journaling habit is a mindset of gracious flexibility. In some cases, just make adjustments to do what you can, given the circumstances. Maybe you shorten your journaling practice to take less time. Perhaps you journal aloud using the voice recorder on your phone while you drive to work. Maybe you defer your journaling to your lunch break. Or maybe, you skip a day or two. None of this should cause guilt or give reason to abandon your commitment. Life happens in unexpected ways. That's normal. Simply return to the practice as soon as you are able, without guilt or shame.

Spiritual growth is about real life, not some idealized life that doesn't fit into your current circumstances. Any spiritual practice that doesn't allow gracious flexibility for the unpredictability of life is too brittle to survive.

PRACTICE

◆ **Journal on your preconceptions regarding habit building.**

Use any of these prompts:

- What's your experience with building new habits? Where have you had the most success? What have been your most frequent obstacles?

- Before reading today's entry, what was your perspective on missing a day when it comes to any life-change-oriented habit? How has this perspective on missing a day impacted your habit-building?

- How does it feel to hear it's possible to build habits without holding yourself to an impossible standard of perfection? What possibilities does this open for you?

TIME & SPACE

READ & REFLECT

As we turn to the more tangible tools for journaling, keep our first tool in mind. Gracious flexibility will enable you to stick with journaling for the long haul. Certain choices may serve your goals better, yet dogmatic inflexibility will undermine your progress. Nothing impedes building a habit more than the drive to have everything "just so." (Also true for spiritual maturity.)

How long?

The matter of how much time to spend journaling is simple. Spend as much time as you need within the confines of the time you have. Reflection is your goal. That takes time. Even so, we all live in the tension between our ideals and what we can sustain.

It's tough to do this process in less than fifteen minutes. For many beginners, fifteen to thirty minutes is a good place to start. As you gain experience you'll develop an instinct for how much time you need. As you grow comfortable with the process, you'll notice time goes by quickly. In different seasons of life you'll need more or less time. In some very difficult times, for example, I've needed journaling sessions that lasted a couple of hours! In my current practice, I usually plan on about forty-five minutes to give me what I need, but if my schedule is pressing, I can get by with less.

Your practice needs to be sustainable for your life. So, keep this rule in mind: Spend as much time as you need within the confines of the time you have.

When?

Part of deciding how much time to spend is determining when you have time available. Christians are often taught to spend devotional time first thing in the morning, but no particular time is more spiritual than any other. The best time for you is the time you'll most likely stick with.

Early morning offers particular benefits. You can center yourself before starting down the train track of your day's agenda. When I journal in the morning regularly, my mindset throughout the day is more gentle and flexible. I feel more aware of God in and around me. For many of us, though, morning practices are difficult because of our morning rush. If you struggle to wake up and get yourself moving or have other early morning commitments, then forcing a practice of reflection into that same window of time won't likely work.*

Journaling at the end of the day provides different benefits. Your work has come to an end. The day's experiences are still fresh. Ending your day with spiritual focus and reflection can help settle your mind and heart for rest, unless you're too tired to think and you fall asleep in the middle of reflection.

Where at?

Choose a location that supports consistency and sustainability. This is more important than working to find or create the perfect, peaceful environment. You can easily undermine your new habit by having too strict a view of the environment you need to have a spiritual experience. There are too many ways your perfect mental image can be disrupted. Instead of settling into the practice, you'll be frustrated that you can't do it the way you want.

The space that works best will be determined by your personality, the season of life you're in, and the options available to you. I love journaling in coffee shops. Being away from home and office allows me to disconnect from the piles that inevitably collect there. The background buzz of the coffee shop helps me focus. Others find this distracting. I also journal at my kitchen table in the morning. When my kids were little, this had to be very early in the morning when the house was still. When my kids were older and my mental health made getting up early difficult, I sat down to journal once the kids were on their way to

---

* For some of us it's worth considering whether our rushed morning may mean we're not stewarding our evenings in such a way as to give ourselves the best chance of an effective morning. It took me years to accept this reality: The success of my morning is often determined the night before. Short version: healthy sleep patters matter.

school. That white table by the window, a cup of Earl Grey, and forty-five minutes become a sacred space for me.

I've had to make adjustments to my space and time over the years. This kind of flexibility is key to keeping the habit going. Your life is different from mine. Choose a place where you can be relatively undistracted, other obligations generally won't intrude, and you feel comfortable. Most importantly, choose a place you have regular access to. Then have a backup option!* Your new habit will take root more quickly if you can be consistent, but always hold your preferences with gracious flexibility.

---

* You may have already noticed that making these decisions means thinking about the expectations and needs of your family or housemates. Many of us live in shared spaces that we can't expect to be in exactly the condition we prefer with others who don't follow our schedules. Part of building a sustainable habit of journaling may include negotiating some space and time with those you live with.

PRACTICE

◆ **In a journal entry, consider the time and space that might best support you in developing a long-term habit of journaling.**

- **Review your current routine and schedule to identify both a time and length of time you think you could commit to this practice.**

- **Are there changes you might need to make to clear a regular window of time?**

- **Reflect on what factors would help you enjoy the process and more quickly focus.**

  - When during the day do you have the most mental focus?

  - What kind of environment would you most enjoy?

  - Where are spaces like this available in your life?

  - What changes might you need to make to have these spaces or environments available?

  - Do you think morning or evening would work better for you over the long run?

Later I'll ask you to make a commitment to a specific time, length, and location, but for now, just reflect on the possibilities that might be the best for you.

As you look at your life, you may honestly find that it feels impossible to fit in a journaling practice. If that's the case, you may need to push pause on this book and take a look at the larger issue of how to be a spiritual person in the midst of a busy life. This is a common reality these days I'm frequently asked to address. I wrote a 10-week online course to help people in this situation. It's called *Not Just One More Thing: Spiritual Growth for Busy People.* You can learn more about this at http://live210.com/too-busy/.

FREQUENCY & FAITHFULNESS

READ & REFLECT

The next important ingredient to consider is frequency. You already know habits take root best with frequent repetition. Journaling every day, every other day, five days a week, or another high-frequency routine is the best way to build this habit.* For some of us, though, a commitment to journal every day can be an obstacle to a sustainable practice.

I'm not the only one with a vein of perfectionism, legalism,† or performance-based value-building running through my soul. If you're like me then making the commitment to journal daily will seem like the right choice. It shows we're serious! Fueled by enthusiasm, we'll keep our appointment for a while. We might start to feel a bit proud of ourselves, maybe even spiritually superior.

Then we miss a day or two (inevitable!) and that pendulum of inner judgment swings the other way. Now we're not keeping our commitment. That doesn't feel good. We double down but life has other plans. Again, we miss a day or a few and our commitment starts to feel impossible. Those feelings of failure lead us to distance from the practice even more. Add enough guilt and shame and we will abandon the practice entirely.

I've lived this cycle many times. Maybe you have, too. It took me quite a while to learn that these feelings are not about the practice. They are emotional responses to experiences that seem to threaten our internal sense of success. For some of us, that

---

* This is backed by clinical studies. If you're interested, you can find more in Appendix 5: Literature on Habit Building.

† In the context of religion, legalism refers to a religious system that is transactional. Legalists are those who believe that they can build or demonstrate merit by keeping God's law. For some, this accumulated merit can earn salvation. For others, it is the way to access Divine blessing or even prosperity. Legalism can extend beyond moral behavior to right belief as well. In every version, the believer is obliged to fulfill the law of God, often with an implied assumption that in return, God is obliged to grant favor and blessing.

feeling is crucial for our identity. Performance becomes a way to feel secure, worthy, and accepted. If you add a sense of spiritual obligation to this performance drive, it makes things so much worse! You might feel you're not just failing your own good intentions, you're also failing God! That's a heavy and unnecessary burden.

If you struggle with this mindset, I recommend two things. First, be very gentle with yourself regarding how frequently you journal. It is counter-productive to wage an internal battle with guilt or shame when you miss a day. Your inner critic is not a trustworthy guide for spiritual growth. Until we do our healing work, most of us find our desire to build a new habit is not strong enough to beat out shame. Keep the principle of gracious flexibility always before you.

Second, instead of seeing this performance drive as an obstacle, realize that it provides you with a ready topic to process in your journal! Why does missing a day or even a few days stir up these feelings in you? Why do you relate to performance in this way? If you're anything like me, there is much to be gained by walking with the Spirit through these inner struggles.

If you miss a day because of a crisis at work, come back to your practice the next day. If you get sick and need extra sleep, return to your practice when you're feeling better. If you take a week-long vacation with your family and want to give your full attention to being present to them, great! Hold your practice with gracious flexibility and return to it when you get back.

Journal most days, as often as you reasonably can. This is the best path forward, so long as you remember our goal. Checking off boxes of accomplishment does not lead to personal or spiritual growth. Faithfulness does. So, despite the complexities of your life, your varying levels of motivation, and inevitable interruptions, keep returning. This faithfulness is the precious raw material of spiritual growth.*

---

* Just in case, because someone is bound to misunderstand: Faithfulness, here, does not mean perfection. It means that you keep coming back.

PRACTICE

◆ **Journal about the matter of frequency.**

Use any or all of the following prompts.

- If you've had a past experience with journaling, what was your attitude toward frequency? How did this attitude impact your experience?

- Is a drive to perform or accomplish part of your make-up? If so, how might this shape your goal of building a sustainable practice?

- Considering your current life and commitments, what frequency seems like a reasonable starting point? Daily? Five days a week? Three days a week? Why does this frequency seem right for you?

PEN & PAPER, KEYS & SCREENS

READ & REFLECT

Today we turn to the tools you thought were the most important—what you write with. You have two paths. The analog choice of pen or pencil and paper, or the digital option of keyboard and screen.[*]

Which should you use? The one that works best for you. Which will be more accessible? Which will engage your mind more? Which will you enjoy? You'll more quickly build a habit by picking a single set of tools and sticking with it. Both the analog and digital paths have advantages and disadvantages.[†]

An analog journal?

Writing longhand in a notebook has a classic feel. For some, this seems more sacred and weighty than a screen. Unlike your computer, a paper journal has a single purpose. It has no other apps or notifications to break your focus. Also, most of us type faster than we write. The slowness of handwriting might feel frustrating, but it can shift you into a more present mind. That slower, more reflective mode may make it easier to notice your feelings, thoughts, and even the Spirit.

On the other hand, in our digital culture, writing longhand can be intimidating. A word written in ink feels like a commitment, like you have to get it right. If you spent time

---

[*] Variations like a stylus on a screen, voice memo, or even an old-fashioned typewriter notwithstanding.

[†] If you're already experienced with journaling, you may already know your preference. If that's the case, then allow today's entry to be an opportunity to think about the reasons why you prefer one or the other. A successful journaling practice requires that every element—even something as prosaic as the tools you use—is intentional. Trying a different experience might give you new insights about your practice. If you'd rather stick with what you already are comfortable with, do it but with reflection, so you understand how your choice impacts your experience.

choosing the perfect journal, you might struggle to actually write words because you don't want to spoil it with messy handwriting.

A digital journal?

As our lives move increasingly into the digital world, it can make sense to journal there as well. For many, our devices are constantly within reach, which means our journal is also with us. It's much easier to build a habit when you have the instruments immediately at hand!

Digital journaling has its own benefits, whether in a mobile app or in a word processing document. Your journal never runs out of pages. Searching past entries is effortless. Most digital journals can be password-protected. For some, the speed of typing can overcome one of the biggest hurdles to journaling—the time it takes.

On the other hand, the computer or device can itself be a distraction. Notifications, social media, and work-related applications can intrude. Something more entertaining or more urgent is a single click or tap away. If you find yourself easily distracted, a paper journal may be the better route.*

Whether you journal on paper or screen, set yourself up for success by making sure your devices can't interrupt you. Turn off notifications. Put your phone into Do Not Disturb mode or turn it off. Your world will survive the thirty or sixty minutes you're away, and so will you. In fact, you'll be better for it.

---

* Although if you're committed to digital journaling, there are ways to limit the distractions. I've made some recommendations in Appendix 3: Recommended Tools.

PRACTICE

◆ **Consider whether analog or digital is right for you.**

- **Which option will best help you build a sustainable habit? In your journal, consider the following:**
  - Which mode will be more easily available to you? Which will you enjoy using more?
  - Are you particularly distractible? Is typing speed an issue for you? Or maybe your handwriting?
  - Do you have accessibility needs that would make one choice or the other better for you?

◆ **Procure the tools you've decided on.**

Whichever path you choose, gather your tools so that you can begin using your new journal as we work toward building your habit in the coming pages.

- **If you're going analog:**
  - Pick up a journal.
  - Find a pen or pencil that writes comfortably.
  - I've listed some of my favorites with commentary and links in Appendix 3: Recommended Tools.
- **If you're going digital:**
  - Find a journaling tool that works for you. This could be a simple word processing document in your favorite word processor, or one of the many great apps designed for journaling.
  - Review my favorites with some commentary, recommendations, and links in Appendix 3: Recommended Tools.

THE KEY THAT OPENS THE DOOR

READ & REFLECT

Today we address one last tool you need: an essential mindset. Remember, this isn't a guide to journaling in general. We're working to build a habit of journaling *for spiritual growth*. Spiritual growth will happen because you come to the process with a spiritual intention.

This practice doesn't require you to hold particular theology, belong to a certain denomination, or even identify as a Christian. People with varying religious identities have used this process and found it helpful.

How do we bring a spiritual intention to the practice? We start with trust.* We trust that God—in whatever way we presently understand the Divine—is active and present. We journal with an expectation that God can speak. If "speak" seems too concrete, use language that works for you. Come with the expectation that, in some way, God can lead or influence your inner life. You don't have to understand how this works. You don't need a clear matrix to discern the difference between your thoughts and God's.

What's necessary is a baseline trust that you are not alone, that God is with you, and that God is working for your healing and growth.† If it makes more sense to you, substitute the word faith for trust. Or, if faith and trust still seem beyond your grasp,

---

* Perhaps you're already comfortable with the idea of "hearing from God." If that's the case, some of my explanations may seem elementary. Even so, I'd like to invite you to consider the framing I offer. I also grew up in church and learned many different religious and spiritual practices at a young age, but what I share here comes from a different starting point. We're not doing this from obligation or legalism. We're not doing it because it's the proscribed practice of our particular theological stream. We're starting from a commitment to trust. Everything grows from there.

† If this is new for you, or you come from a Christian tradition that doesn't talk about this, take some time to read and reflect on my essay, "What Is Spiritual Growth?" in Appendix 1.

simply hold hope that God is present. That's enough. I think you already have that hope; it's why you picked up this book.

Starting with trust that God is present changes the nature of journaling. Now, you're not just expressing your own thoughts. You're also listening. Expecting God's presence and influence moves you away from self-indulgence into the realm of humility. A posture of trust implies that you are not an expert in living. In the ancient Hebrew Scripture, David wrote: "Search me, God, and know my heart; test me and know my concerns."* Trust is the key that opens the door to spiritual growth.

Even the physical action of journaling can become a fruitful spiritual discipline. Consider the meaning of each action. You carve out time, even when other obligations are pressing. You prioritize an activity most people around you won't understand, and the prevailing culture does not reward. You sit in a real place, taking real time, using your hands and words to focus your mind and heart. And then, you keep coming back, even when it doesn't feel amazing. With these simple choices, you exercise embodied trust.† Doing so disciplines your body and mind.‡

Your humble and faithful practice opens up a recurring space of silence in your life where Spirit can speak. Of course, Spirit is always moving and speaking, but we rarely allow the stillness necessary to notice. In the quiet, reflective space of your journal, you practice being present. By faithful repetition, you are building spiritual muscles that have atrophied in our culture of speed, self-gratification, and image management. You are attending to the Spirit. What you practice becomes more natural.

In the coming days, we'll talk about how to use this time, but what makes the process effective isn't certain steps you take or the words you write. If you maintain a habit of journaling over time, you'll find the shape of the habit will necessarily evolve. In

---

* Psalms 139, various versions.

† Ben Sternke and Matt Tebbe offer a useful definition of belief as "embodied trust." They wrote, "We learn to dwell in love through embodied, experiential participation. Our participation in God's life happens...by taking steps of trust with our bodies." *Having the Mind of Christ: Eight Axioms to Cultivate a Robust Faith.* Intervarsity Press; Downers Grove, IL 2022. 138

‡ Some think the word *discipline* is about punishment. It's not. It's about experiential learning. The old word *disciple* is most equivalent to *apprentice*. It's the process of learning by doing.

different seasons of your life, you may spend more or less time. You may include more scripture or less, or even none. At times, you may focus more on the narrative of your life. Other times, the focus may shift to understanding your emotions. You might include elements like a prayer list or a gratitude list.

Even as the structure of your journal changes, this essential mindset remains the same. Enter into your journaling with an expectation of God's presence and a commitment to listen. Doing this elevates journaling into a spiritual practice.

PRACTICE

◆ **Journal through your response to this premise.**

The central necessity that makes this journaling process spiritual is an expectation that God is present and can guide or influence you.

- **Is this an easy idea for you to accept or not? Why do you think that is?**

- **Think about your current understanding of and relationship with God. Briefly, how would you define it?**

- I invited you to start with an attitude of trust. I also suggested that if it's helpful you could substitute the word faith or even hope. **Which of these three words (trust, faith, hope) are you most comfortable using when you think about God's presence and influence in your life? Why do you choose that word?**

UNDERSTAND THE ESSENTIAL INGREDIENTS

Flour, yeast, water, and salt. Those four ingredients make bread. Other things can be added, of course. Cultures around the world have started with these simple ingredients and transformed them into so many wonderful things.

In the same way, your journaling can include many different ingredients. There are endless variations and additions that can change the flavor or adapt the practice to your current needs. Yet a core set of ingredients are required. Understanding these essential ingredients will keep your journaling process on track for a long-term, sustainable practice that results in spiritual growth.

The Spine

Read & Reflect

How many ways can you eat an Oreo? Dip it in milk. Unscrew the wafers and lick the frosting. (Barbarian!) One at a time? By the sleeve? No matter how you eat it, what makes an Oreo stays the same. There are many ways to journal for spiritual growth. Longer or shorter sessions. Paper or screen. More, less, or even no scripture. Different kinds of prayer. Gratitude lists. Reflections on relationships, emotions, work issues, or the kids. Wrestling with theology. Your process will evolve, but the core should stay the same.

These core ingredients form a spine that gives your practice form. Without them, your journaling will inevitably slump toward some other purpose. I'll introduce them to you now and in the coming days we'll look more closely at each.

Silence

The first ingredient is silence. The blank page or screen may seem like a prompt to create, to make words. Instead, see the blank page as a tangible reminder to listen. We will write words, but we're after the kind of authentic and helpful words that only emerge from reflective silence. We are children of an image-infatuated culture saturated in polished propaganda and marketing. Silence is resistance. Starting here, we begin to wean ourselves away from our inclination to use words to defend, justify, and control.

Inward Reflection

The second ingredient is reflection on our inner world. This is the meta-cognition I mentioned earlier. When we journal, we're not just writing down what's happened or even how we feel about it. We're observing what we think and feel *about* what we think and feel. Journaling improves our ability to learn from the experience of being ourselves.

Godward Reflection

The third ingredient is reflection on God's character and presence.* Understanding ourselves is necessary for growth, but humility reminds us that we are part of a larger whole. If our goal is spiritual growth, then our attention must turn away from self toward reality greater than ourselves. For me, this is God. There are various ways to do this. We'll talk about that in due time. Turning our attention toward God protects us from getting lost in our own self-justifying mythology.

Prayer

The fourth ingredient is prayer. That's a loaded word that can mean many things depending on your background. I use the word here to remind you that your journal is not a monologue. In your journal, you're reflecting on life, circumstances, and your inner world with an expectation that Spirit is present and has something to say. By including some element of prayer, we remind ourselves that we are not alone in the universe. Our prayer is an act of trust that God cares about our healing, growth, and relationship with the world.

Of course, each of these ingredients can stand alone. Combined in the context of journaling, something profound happens. We're not just practicing silence to find greater peace, although that will happen. We're not just reflecting on our lives so we can know ourselves better. We're not reflecting on God to improve our theology. We're not praying because that's just something religious people do. These ingredients train us to live in ongoing dialogue with Spirit. We practice being conscious of the present moment, the one place where God can be found.†

---

* This part of the process matters, even if you're not sure about God right now. We are reflecting on that which is greater than us. You might think of it as Ultimate Reality or Love. Reflecting on something larger than us can offer some protection from the precious self-justifying stories we construct about ourselves.

† You and I live our lives "on the timeline," so to speak. We are conscious of the past, present, and future, but only move forward one moment at a time. In most views, God exists above, beyond, or outside of time. If this is true, then there is only one place where our finite human lives intersect with the infinite Divine life. That sacred place is this one present moment. This is why learning to be fully present in the moment is such an essential spiritual practice.

Over time this practice provides another important benefit. When I was young, my family had a spot on the kitchen wall where my parents would mark off the kids' height each year. Those hatch marks were so important for me. Without them, it was hard to notice that I was growing. Spiritual growth is similarly hard to see. In our journal we build a record of our spiritual growth. Looking back at older entries I can see ways my perspective has changed. My journal makes it possible to see ways God was working that were too subtle to notice at the time. My journal has become a record and confirmation of God's presence.

Your journaling practice will evolve. You'll add new elements and remove others based on your current needs. As change happens make sure to keep these four ingredients in the mix. This spine provides structure that will keep your practice healthy.

PRACTICE

Each day so far I've provided a prompt for reflection. You've not officially started the full journaling process, but if you've been using these prompts daily, then you're already practicing. As we look more closely at the four core ingredients, I'll provide brief journaling prompts at the end of each reading. All that's left is to start. The most important learning happens in the experience.

One of the biggest obstacles to building a habit of journaling is our own expectations. We expect something mystical to happen. We hope for more than just thinking, writing, and praying. Lay those expectations aside.

I've had profound realizations even a few mystical experiences while journaling, but God is not a vending machine. God doesn't seem to care much about goosebumps or other outward manifestations. Just keep coming back faithfully, holding your practice in gracious flexibility. The process is sacred and important in itself. Trust that God is present and speaking.

◆ **Using the tools you've decided on, at the place and time you've chosen, begin to journal.**

Today, follow this simple sequence:

- **Settle into your space and time for journaling with your tools at hand.** You'll need a timer of some sort as well. The one on your phone is great, *if you turn off notifications.*

- **Sit quietly for one minute.** If your mind won't rest, simply breathe in and out deeply. Slowly count each breath. One on the inhale. Two on the exhale. Continue until ten. If your mind is still buzzing, do it again. If your mind wanders, return to counting breaths. After a minute, proceed.

- **In your journal, reflect briefly on this question:**

  - *What are you hoping to get out of the experience of journaling?*

  - If you're spending 15 minutes total, give 5 minutes to this question. If you're spending 30 minutes, give 10 minutes to this question.

- **Next, write out the words of Psalms 1:1-3, then reflect on this question:**

  - *How can reflecting on God's character and ways make you like a "Tree planted by a stream?"*

  - Spend 5 minutes on this reflection if you're spending 15 minutes total, longer if you have more time.

- **End with a 3-sentence closing prayer following these prompts:**

  - *God, You are . . .*

  - *God, I hear . . .*

  - *God, I will . . .*

Silence

Read & Reflect

Listening is essential for spiritual growth. The painful truth is that most of us are not practiced listeners. Forgive me this direct challenge: Most of us don't listen well because we are not comfortable with silence. We use words to manage others, to control how they feel about us. At times, we listen only to formulate a response. These reactive words are often only self-justifications or ways to move our agenda forward. This is not real listening.

Real listening is an act of humility. When we listen we de-center ourselves so we can hear the truth of another. That's why there is no intimacy without listening.* Similarly, real listening moves us from a transactional understanding of God to an experiential relationship with God. A transactional religious life doesn't require listening. Simply do or say or believe the right thing in the right way. Having done that, we expect God to act on our behalf. We did our bit, now God's supposed to save us, or answer our prayer, or give us the peace we long for. This is God-as-Vending-Machine theology.

The process of journaling for spiritual growth encourages us to shift away from grocery-list prayers toward something that encompasses all of life. When we practice sitting in silence, we learn how to slow the racing mind. We discover mental distraction is often a habit.† When we sit in true silence we become present to what's happening in mind and body. (Some of us begin to see how much energy we've invested in *not* noticing

---

* Interpersonal Neurobiology says this same thing in more technical language. We are more able to attach when we experience safe, agenda-less presence.

† This is true for most minds, but the matter is more complex with cognitive differences like ADD, ADHD, or for those who experience the kinds of intrusive thoughts that can be part of PTSD or other mental health conditions. In these cases, struggles with focus or intrusive thoughts may require professional support.

those things.) Silence opens our inner ear to God's voice, training us to move beyond reading scripture for information that supports our viewpoint. Most importantly, practicing silence changes how we understand prayer. We learn that prayer may use words at times, but when we trust God's presence, all the silence is prayer as well.

This kind of listening is not easy. We use our words to get what we want. Constant clanging media barrage us. Even our inner life jangles with feelings, images, and words. Finding silence requires both interior and exterior intentionality.

Exterior intentionality is easier to manage. It's hard to listen while rushing. Scheduling time to journal stops the usual rush for a window of time. It's also hard to listen over the noise of distractions. So make a quiet space. Turn off your nagging devices, and do what you can to minimize other intrusions. Finding interior silence is much more challenging. Our minds spin, rushing off to the next worry, intrigue, or imagination. The Spirit whispers. It takes practice to still the noise of heart and mind. Until this habit has taken root, doers hate sitting in silence. To them, it feels an impossible waste of time. It's not. Silence opens our inner world.

How do we include silence in the process of journaling? In the upcoming days, and in Appendix 4: Ways to Practice, you'll find several options you can try. Here are two simple starting points.

BEGIN WITH SILENCE

Before you write anything, sit in silence. A minute may be all you can handle at first. If you're new to this practice, your mind will actively resist it. You'll remember an urgent task. You'll feel a desperate mental itch to handle "just this one thing." Now that you're trying to be still, your mind will present any excuse to force you back into the comforting distraction of busyness.

All of this is a trick, a literal mind-game. The thinking self we call the mind is desperate to avoid silence. Why? Because silence gives the ego nothing to work with. In silence, we forgo the words we use to get our way and curate our image. We set aside the words that define our sense of identity. Each moment of silence is a moment you are not justifying or labeling yourself, positioning yourself over and against others, declaring your agenda, or voicing your worries. Each moment of silence is a tiny death of self. Without that noise, what will you hear? Who will you be?

This is why most of us cannot bear more than a minute or two of true silence. Practice will increase both your capacity and your enjoyment. It is a great relief to finally learn you can exist without the constant chatter of self-justification or self-condemnation. Starting with silence allows you to come into your journaling with a mind ready for reflection. Silence opens your inner ears.

You can begin training yourself for silence by focusing on your breath. This practice gives you a tangible way to set aside the buzz of thought and ground yourself in the moment.

- **With your eyes closed, breathe in.**
- **Pay attention to the sensation of the air entering your nostrils.**
- **Feel your diaphragm expanding.**
- **Hold the breath for a beat and then slowly breathe out.**
- **Notice the feeling of the air moving out of your body.**
- **Count as you go, saying the numbers in your mind. "One" on the inhale; "Two" on the exhale. "Three" on the inhale; "Four" on the exhale.**
- **Do this until the count of ten.**
- **Then start again, with each breath paying close attention to the sensation of breathing.**

The mental counting provides a focus that keeps noisy thoughts at bay. As your mind settles into silence, you can quiet the counting as well. At a comfortable but slow pace, you should be able to count to ten twice in one minute. After practicing for a while, you'll be able to do the breathing exercise without counting and your mind will naturally settle.[*]

---

[*] This is called Diaphragmatic Breathing and it has surprising benefits. Learn more here: https://live210.com/breathing/

If you prefer to use words rather than counting, the Jesus Prayer works well. The Jesus prayer is an Eastern Orthodox breath prayer,* used by Christians since at least the 5th century. As you breathe in, pray in your mind, "Lord Jesus Christ, Son of God . . ." As you breathe out, pray, ". . . have mercy on me, a sinner."† At a comfortable, slow pace, you should be able to repeat the Jesus Prayer about ten times in a minute. Again, once your mind settles, continue breathing without words for a period.

INCLUDE SILENT MARGINS

The second simple way to incorporate silence into your journaling practice is to include silence throughout. Notice the white space in this book, the margins that surround the text and the space between the lines. That white space carries no content. Is it without value? Picture this page of text with no margins, no space between the lines or the words. Just imagining it is stressful! The white space makes the words intelligible.

In the same way, you can include silence as a margin between parts of your journaling process. Add fifteen seconds, thirty seconds, even a minute of silence between each element. If you are reflecting on scripture or writing a response to a prompt, pause in silence before starting to write. As you write, pause between sentences or even after a thought. This silent pause breaks the natural inclination to fill all the space. It also keeps your mind in a listening posture.

The more you practice, the more the slow pace of expectant silence will come to feel familiar and welcome. You'll grow in your capacity to set aside your agenda, your own self-soothing words, even your urgency to move on to the next thing. That's when you will have begun to listen.

----

* A prayer short enough to be prayed in the span of a breath in and out.

† Don't let the word "sinner" in this ancient prayer derail you. This is not inviting self-flagellation or pushing shame. It's simply acknowledging our human weakness. The request for mercy is a recognition that every good gift comes from God. With these words the Jesus Prayer orients us. We need mercy. We need the good only God can provide. And if, for whatever reason, those words aren't helpful to you, then by all means, don't use them. An interesting explanation of the meaning and use of the Jesus Prayer can be found here: https://live210.com/jesus-prayer/

PRACTICE

◆ **Journal, following this simple sequence.**

- **Settle into your space and time for journaling, tools at hand.** You'll also need a one-minute timer. Put your devices into Do Not Disturb mode.

- **Begin with silence, as described above.** If you're new to sitting in silence, start with one minute. If you need help setting aside the noise in your mind, focus on your breathing or use the Jesus Prayer.

- **Reflect briefly in your journal:**
  - *What did this period of silence feel like?*
    - *What did you notice in your mind and body?*
    - *Why do you think you had this experience with silence today?*
  - Spend up to a third of your time here.

- **Write out Psalms 62:5 in your journal, then reflect on this question:**
  - *How often do you have intentional silence in your life?*
  - *Do you naturally tend to seek silence or avoid it? Why do you think this is?*
  - *How might silence help you hear or connect with God?*
  - Spend at least a third of your total time here.

- **End with a 3-sentence closing prayer following these prompts:**
  - *God, You are . . .*
  - *God, I hear . . .*
  - *God, I will . . .*

WEEK 3, DAY 3

INWARD REFLECTION

READ & REFLECT

In the simplest terms, inward reflection means thinking about our thoughts. We consider what we think and why. We examine how we've responded to circumstances and interactions through emotions, thoughts, and actions. We reflect on the outcomes and consequences of those responses. With the Spirit's guidance, we notice whether our responses align with who we want to be as people or who we believe God invites us to be. This is one way we come to know ourselves.

The ancient Hebrew Scriptures encourage us, "Let us test and examine our ways."* Psalm 139 provides a model prayer: "Search me, O God, and know my heart; test me and know my thoughts. See if there is any wicked way in me, and lead me in the way everlasting."† Conscious of God's presence—or at least trusting the possibility of God's presence—we can more easily discern that some of our thoughts, responses, and habits lead us into pain, sickness, or bondage, while others lead to flourishing.

Depending on your background, you may find this emphasis on self-reflection unexpected. You may have been taught that thinking about yourself is wrong or selfish. Certainly, there is a risk of becoming self-absorbed. Yet, spiritual growth causes us to move more and more toward a truthful picture of ourselves. Another ancient prayer from Hebrew scripture describes a person seeking God. "I have promised to keep Your words. I have sought Your favor with all my heart . . . I thought about my ways and turned my steps back to Your decrees."‡ This person wants to know God. Yet notice! To follow God well, they had to think about their ways.

---

* Lamentations 3:40, NRSV.

† Psalms 139:23-24, NRSV.

‡ Psalm 119:57-59, NIV.

The trouble is that we think we know ourselves. Most of us don't. The longer we live in a state of noise and rush, the less we know ourselves. We ignore the trending direction of our thoughts, emotions, and responses. We rarely observe who we are becoming.

Until we practice inward reflection, we remain caught in the press of urgency. Our inner world is a constantly changing geography of thoughts, emotions, hopes, and expectations. This landscape is shaped by our experience, our beliefs, and the story we tell about our lives. It contains the deep well of our secrets, our fears, and our dreams. This inner world informs our will. It is also where we meet the Spirit.

There are many different ways to reflect on our inner world. The best way for you will depend on your current season and where you sense growth or healing is necessary. Next week I'll suggest several ideas, and there are even more options in Appendix 4 you might find helpful.

For many years, the focus of growth and healing in my life was my emotions. In my woundedness and emotional immaturity, I was hurting people around me. Because of this focus, my daily journaling included reflecting on my emotions. Your story is different than mine. Your reflections will, of course, be different, too. Regardless of the specific focus, your goal in your journal is to enter this inner place accompanied by God's gracious presence so that you can see yourself more truly.

PRACTICE

◆ **Journal following this simple template:**

- **Settle yourself and begin with silence.**
- **Reflect briefly in your journal:**
  - *What did you notice happening in your thoughts or emotions as you read today's entry?*
    - *Did you feel excitement or resistance?*
    - *What questions, if any, come up?*
    - *Why do you think you had that response?*
  - Spend a third of your time on this reflection.
- **Write out Psalm 139:23-24 in your journal, then follow this prompt:**
  - *Write your own version of Psalm 139, using your words to make each line your own.*
  - *How will you invite the Spirit of God to be part of your journaling process?*
  - *What do you want to learn about yourself and why?*
  - Spend at least a third of your total time on this reflection.
- **End with a 3-sentence closing prayer following these prompts:**
  - *God, You are . . .*
  - *God, I hear . . .*
  - *God, I will . . .*

GODWARD REFLECTION

READ & REFLECT

Are you surprised the process of journaling for spiritual growth does not begin by focusing on God? We begin with silence and inward reflection. Starting elsewhere is an exercise in denial. You exist in a body. Your body moves through experiences. You perceive and understand those experiences through your senses, emotions, and thoughts. Often those emotions and thoughts are only reactive. Silence allows us to notice and slow these reactions so we can be present to ourselves, others, and the world with compassion.

Only once we've settled ourselves can we enter into patient interior attention, and only then can we profitably reflect on God. You might argue the point with me. You might say you've read scripture or thought about God without starting in silence and interior reflection. I know, I have too. The trouble is that we all live in grave risk of thinking thoughts about God shaped by our projections and urgent needs. Religious practices like prayer, study, or even contemplation can become an exercise in underwriting self-justification.

Even when we read scripture or theology, which our western rationalist heritage suggests are the most objective ways to know God, we perceive those words through the filters of our own story, thoughts, and feelings. This is inescapable.* How crucial it is, then, that we are humble and circumspect. Thinking and talking about God without a chastened sense of our own limited

---

* Consider the insight of Dr. James Cone on this subject: "Because Christian theology is human speech about God, it is always related to historical situations, and thus all of its assertions are culturally limited . . . Although God, the subject of theology, is eternal, theology itself is, like those who articulate it, limited by history and time...[Our image of God] is a finite image, limited by the temporality and particularity of our existence. Theology is not universal language; it is interested language and thus is always a reflection of the goals and aspirations of a particular people in a definite social setting." Cone, James. *God of the Oppressed*. Orbis Press; New York 1997. 39.

perspective will always lead to the construction of self-justifying idols. Silence and truthful self-reflection help us practice this necessary humility.

Having set this stage, we can now turn to reflect on God, God's nature, and God's work in our lives. The Apostle Paul gave us a helpful guide:

> Whatever is true, whatever is honorable, whatever is just, whatever is pure, whatever is lovely, whatever is commendable—if there is any moral excellence and if there is any praise—dwell on these things.[*]

This passage is often used to measure what kind of media, books, or conversations are worthwhile, but that's reductive. This passage is most helpful as an invitation to reflect on the qualities of the Divine nature. God is true when so much of life is false. God is honorable when so many are not worthy of respect. God is just in the face of humanity's injustice. God is pure, excellent, and praiseworthy when life[†] is anything but.

John's gospel refines our vision further. "Love is from God; everyone who loves is born of God and knows God. Whoever does not love does not know God, for God is love."[‡] The ancient Hebrews (and modern Judaism which descends from them) understood God this way: "You are a God ready to forgive, gracious and merciful, slow to anger and abounding in steadfast love."[§] The early Christians, familiar with the ancient Hebrew vision, saw this love embodied in Jesus. They recorded Jesus saying, "Whoever has seen me has seen the Father."[**]

When we spend time reflecting on God in these terms, our understanding of love, justice, holiness, and truth grows clearer. We see better what it means to be godly.[††] Holding God's nature in mind serves as a compass for where we're headed and as the

---

[*] Philippians 4:8, CSB.

[†] Including religion and religious people.

[‡] 1 John 4:7-8, NRSV.

[§] Nehemiah 9:17, NRSV.

[**] John 14:9, NRSV.

[††] Literally "like God."

measure of who we want to be. As we return to this reflection time and again, we change.

Spiritual growth, however, is not only about maturing as a person. It is also, and more importantly, about entering into a life shaped by that which is true, honorable, just, pure, lovely, commendable, morally excellent, praise-worthy, gracious, merciful, slow to anger and abounding in steadfast love, or more directly put, a life shaped like God.

There are many ways to go about this. Next week and in Appendix 4 you'll find a number of suggestions. We can begin with scripture. We may study the text or we may read looking for a point of entry—a character we relate to, words that connect with our lives. Often, the most profitable path is to just read and re-read, slowly letting the words sow something in us subconsciously. Scripture memorization has been an unexpected gift, as I've found that the more familiar I am with the words, the more I can simply reflect and listen. Other insightful spiritual work, like thoughtful poetry, song, and spiritual memoir, can also guide our reflection.

Regardless of how we focus our thoughts onto God and God's nature, keeping Godward reflection in the journaling process invites us deeper into maturity and relationship with the Divine.

PRACTICE

◆ **Continue journaling, following a similar template to the past few days.**

- **Settle yourself.**
- **Begin with silence using focusing tools as needed.**
- **Respond to this prompt in your journal:**
  - *Honestly evaluate whether reflecting on God's nature and presence is already a part of your life in any way. If so, how do you do this? If you don't, why do you think that is?*
  - *In what ways do you think that the mental image people hold of God* shapes their lives? How has it shaped yours?*
  - Spend up to a third of your time on this.
- **Next write these words from Nehemiah 9:17: "You are a God ready to forgive, gracious and merciful, slow to anger and abounding in steadfast love."** Then respond to this prompt:
  - *How might your inner life and outer reactions be different if you were to regularly reflect on the qualities of God listed in this passage?*
  - Spend at least a third of your time here.
- **End with a 3-sentence closing prayer following these prompts:**
  - *God, You are . . .*
  - *God, I hear . . .*
  - *God, I will . . .*

---

* Or however they think of Ultimate Reality.

WEEK 3, DAY 5

PRAYER

READ & REFLECT

We most often think of prayer as communication with the Divine. Because most of us don't hear God's voice in an auditory way, we expect a one-sided conversation. We talk, listing off our needs and desires, trusting or hoping that God is listening. How limited. How limiting!

Think of the many forms of communication naturally part of intimate relationships. We may sit face-to-face sharing in hushed voices, glances, or touch. More often, at the kitchen table or in the car, we'll chat about what's happening in our lives. We might leave notes for each other that range from practical to romantic. Many times we sit in the same space, each doing our own thing, confidently resting in the quiet presence of our friend or partner.*

Prayer encompasses all of this. Talking and listening, expressing emotion, asking for needs to be met, reverent formality, and intimate spontaneity all are wrapped in the trusting confidence (or perhaps, hope) that God is present and attentive.

With this in mind, incorporate prayer in your journaling by starting with two assumptions. Consider them steps of faith. First, assume God is present. Second, assume God's Spirit can, in some way that doesn't need to be defined, move or guide you.

What happens when we journal from the vantage of these two assumptions? The entire journaling process becomes prayer! Silence becomes a prayerful ally, subduing our noisy inner monologue so we can more easily acknowledge God's presence.

---

* My friend, Shelley Kehler-Thorpe, helped me see this, pointing out the range of communication in her marriage and comparing this to our prayer life. We don't expect every human interaction or communication to be intense, intimate, and emotional. That's unrealistic and unsustainable. Relationships need other kinds of communication with different intensities, even the kind of communication that happens in shared silence and presence. It's strange to expect that communication with God would not include this same wide range of different purposes, emotional intensity, and styles.

Inward reflection enables us to join with God in seeing ourselves truthfully. Godward reflection opens our hearts for guidance. By the time we begin to do what seems most like prayer—writing words directly addressed to God—we find we've been praying the whole time.

Now we can bring our journaling session to a close with words addressed to God. We are not limited to the "Dear Lord . . . list of things I'm thankful for . . . list of things I need . . . In Jesus' name, Amen" sorts of prayers some of us were taught. There are countless ways to pray. In different seasons of life and with different needs, you'll find different prayers most meaningful. However you do it, bring your journaling to a close by committing yourself to God and God's work in and through you for the day.

With that, we've now seen the spine that gives structure to our journaling: Silence, Inward Reflection, Godward Reflection, and Prayer. Taken together, these four ingredients are what transform journaling into a spiritual practice.

Of course, all four can stand alone, and none require journaling. You've likely done some or all of them in one way or another before. But when they are integrated and expressed in journaling, something much deeper can happen. The tangible process of writing forces a slowed focus that improves and deepens each of these disciplines. This is true whether you're able to journal for just fifteen minutes or an hour.

PRACTICE

◆ **Continue journaling.**

Follow a similar template to the past few days.

- **Settle yourself.**

- **Begin with silence for at least a minute, as before.** If you feel drawn to extend it longer, by all means, do!

- **After silence, respond to this prompt:**
  - *Reflect on the role of prayer in your life to this point.*
    - *Who taught you about prayer?*
    - *Do you pray regularly?*
    - *Has prayer been meaningful to you? Why or why not?*
  - Spend a third of your time on this reflection.

- **Next, copy Philippians 4:6-7 into your journal and then respond to this prompt:**
  - *What does this passage of scripture tell you about God and God's desires for you?*
  - Spend a third of your total time on this reflection.

- **End with a 3-sentence closing prayer following these prompts:**
  - *God, You are . . .*
  - *God, I hear . . .*
  - *God, I will . . .*

WEEK 4

JOURNALING WITH A TEMPLATE

You should have a sense of our purpose now and how journaling for spiritual growth differs from other forms of journaling you may have tried. No matter how helpful the principles or how clear my instruction, though, *doing* is the gateway. You learn to journal by journaling.

This week I'll present a tool that may seem restricting at first: a journal template. Almost universally, people resist this tool when I teach it. Yet, years of experience show that those who use a journaling template are far more likely to build a sustainable habit.

Important Instructions for this week: I'll lead you through several different templates. Plan your week so you'll have the necessary time to experience each one. Day 2 requires a 15-minute window of time. Day 3 takes 30 minutes. Day 4 will take 50 minutes. Even if you already have a length of time in mind that you want to commit to your journaling habit, I want you to experience these different templates so you have a sense of how the process feels with different time constraints. Each template also has a different focus. These templates are examples of how the four essential elements can be blended in various ways to accommodate different lengths of time and spiritual needs.

Each daily entry this week will be brief, just enough information to set you in the right direction. You'll spend your time using the template. On the last day of this week, you'll have a chance to reflect on your experience of the different templates and what you might want to incorporate into your practice.

WEEK 4, DAY 1

WHY USE A TEMPLATE?

READ & REFLECT

I've reminded you so frequently about gracious flexibility that my next words may seem a contradiction. If you're serious about building a habit of journaling you ought to use a template.

A journal template is a predetermined outline for your journaling session.* The template includes the same elements each day. It may even have the same prompts or questions. Every time you journal, you follow your chosen template. If you're journaling long-hand, you might print your template on a separate sheet for reference that you use as a bookmark. If you're journaling on a screen, you can create a template entry or document and then copy it into a new entry for that day.

This may sound limiting but there are several reasons a template is effective. First, the blank page is not your friend. The blank page implies an infinite range of options, but that's not helpful—especially if you have limited time. A template sets your mind in a particular direction.

Second, spiritual growth is not random. Remember the gardening metaphor? The gardener has an outcome in mind. Fresh tomatoes for salsa! As the plants grow, the gardener has a limited set of practices to help move toward her desired outcome —weeding, watering, fertilizing, protecting against pests, disease, and extreme temperature. Gardeners don't employ these tools randomly or by whimsy. They use the right tool that's necessary to nurture the outcome they desire. Personal and spiritual growth works similarly. A template helps you bridge between your long-term intentions and the needs of this present moment.

Third, habits emerge from repetition. Not only do we repeat the habit of sitting down to journal, we also repeat a specific set of elements every time we do it. This builds a kind of internal

---

* If you're a church person, you might think of your template as the "order of service" or the liturgy for your journaling session.

muscle memory. If you're journaling in a new direction every day, some part of your mind will always be preoccupied with the mechanics of the process or where you're headed next. Having a template allows these questions to fade into the background.

Any fear that a template will limit your expression or freedom is misplaced. Over and over, I've watched people who are unwilling to commit to a structure end up abandoning their attempt to build this habit. Trying to force focus takes too much mental and emotional energy. In my experience, the people who stick with this habit over the long haul are exclusively people who use some kind of template or other predetermined routine to structure their journaling time.* Having no structure at all eventually means having no habit.

A template doesn't mean the process should feel stifling. Your template ought to evolve. I make small changes as my needs shift. Every fall, I review my template. Are certain parts no longer helpful? Is there some new area of growth that seems important for me right now? This periodic review allows me to make sure my practice stays vibrant, fresh, and aligned with my intentions and needs. The template isn't a cage, it's a ladder. This is where your commitment to gracious flexibility comes in.

Your template will emerge as you answer these questions:

- **How much time do you have to spend?**

- **How are you going to incorporate silence?**

- **What areas of self-reflection are the most important for you and your personal growth right now?**

---

* Some folks who've been faithfully journaling for years tell me they disagree with my thoughts about using a template. When I've asked them to walk me through their journaling practice, it became quite clear that indeed they had a predetermined structure, they just didn't think of it that way. One woman always wrote a paragraph about the previous day, a paragraph of gratitude, and then a paragraph of prayer, and she never deviated from this pattern. Another person started with an in-depth study of a passage of scripture, then noted ways this scripture connected with their life, and then prayed about what they thought God was teaching them. They had followed this pattern for more than a decade. OK, ditch the word template if you like, but I have yet to meet someone who has stuck with journaling over the long haul who didn't have some basic pattern that they followed. The point is that when you open your journal, you don't have to invent a sense of direction. You already know where you're headed.

- What ways of reflecting on God and God's character seem best for this season of life?

- What prayer practices will be part of your journaling?

- Are there other elements beyond the four essential ingredients you want to include?

The template you begin with will not be the template you use a year from now. On one hand, your template will evolve as you grow, know yourself better, and sense Spirit's direction in your life. On the other hand, your template will provide a structure to keep your journaling habit healthy and on track. When it comes time to build your own template, you'll find a guide to do so in Appendix 2: Building and Evaluating Your Journal Template.

PRACTICE

It may have occurred to you that the short responses last week were a simple template. We'll use that template today.

◆ Continue journaling

Follow a similar template to the past few days.

- **Settle yourself.**
- **Begin with silence using focusing tools as needed.**
- **After silence, respond to this prompt:**
  - *Reflect on your gut response to the idea of a template. Articulate your feelings and then reflect on why you might feel the way you do. What in your story or temperament leads you to that gut response?*
  - Spend a third of your total time here.
- **Copy Matthew 6:9-13 into your journal. You may recognize this as the prayer often called "The Lord's Prayer."** It may not have occurred to you, but this prayer is a template guiding a person through prayer in a series of topical chunks.
  - Once you've copied it, respond to the following prompt: *Identify the topical chunks you see in this prayer. What part of life or spirituality is each chunk focusing on? How might using this template over time shape a person?*
  - Spend at least a third of your time here.
- **End with a 3-sentence closing prayer following these prompts:**
  - *God, You are . . .*
  - *God, I hear . . .*
  - *God, I will . . .*

WEEK 4, DAY 2

THE 15-MINUTE SLOW DOWN

INTRODUCTION

Today's template is simple and short, just fifteen minutes. This doesn't allow much time for going deep, but it's great for someone who has never journaled before. It can also serve if you find yourself in a particularly intense or busy season where your habit feels at risk due to time or energy constraints. Fifteen minutes is about the shortest window that allows you to touch on all four essential elements. This **15-Minute Slow Down** can be a great way to start your day along with coffee and breakfast. It could also easily fit into your lunch break at work.

For a short journaling session like this, you *must* use a timer. Longer templates have room for flexibility, but to fit this process into just 15 minutes, you must monitor your time. The timer on your phone is perfect.[*] If you don't use a timer, the responses will naturally grow longer and your time will expand.

◆ **The 15-Minute Slow Down**

- Gather tools, including a timer, and settle.

Silence (2 minutes)

- Sit in silence for a timed 2 minutes.
- Use focusing tools like counting your breath or the Jesus Prayer as needed.

---

[*] But, Do Not Disturb mode, right?

Reflecting on Your Inner Life (5 minutes)

- Set timer for 5 minutes.

- **Identify an issue or situation that's pressing today.**

  - *In short sentences or bullet points, capture why this feels pressing, what the options are, and its emotional and relational impact.*

- **In a sentence or two, declare who you want to be in relationship to this situation.**

  - This isn't identifying an outcome. It's focusing on character. Something like: "In this situation, I want to be fair" or "In this situation, I refuse to be petty."

Reflecting on God's Character (5 minutes)

- Set timer for 5 minutes.

- **Reflect on the same issue in light of God's character.**

  - *Ask God to guide.*

  - *How might God be present for you in this?*

  - *Who is God inviting you to be?*

Prayer (3 minutes)

- **Sit in silence** for a timed 1 minute.

  - Pay attention to any inward sense of direction.

- **End by writing a closing prayer.**

  - Invite God's guidance for the day.

  - Commit yourself to that guidance.

THE 30-MINUTE GUIDED DEVOTIONAL

INTRODUCTION

Many find thirty minutes a reasonable starting point for a journaling habit. It's long enough not to feel rushed but short enough to fit into most busy lives.

This particular 30-minute template uses a prompt from a devotional book. Countless daily devotional books exist. They usually start with a verse of scripture, followed by a paragraph or two of reflection on that verse, and end with a question for meditation or prayer. The format is so useful that self-help writers, therapists, and other philosophies and religious traditions have adopted it! Starting a journaling habit using a prompt like this is a simple and effective way to begin, especially if you don't know where to begin.

For today's practice, I've provided a devotional below. If you choose to use this template going forward, you'll need to decide on a devotional book to use for your prompt. I've recommended several in the resource list in the Appendix 4: Ways to Practice. You can also use this same template to accompany a scripture reading plan or use of a lectionary.* Instead of a daily devotional, you'd read the daily selection of scripture and then respond to that.

◆ The 30-Minute Guided Devotional

- **Gather your tools**, including a timer, and settle.

Silence (2 minutes)

- **Sit in silence** for a timed 2 minutes.

---

* A lectionary is a tool that schedules the reading of scripture passages to certain weeks of the year. Liturgical church traditions use a lectionary to guide the scripture readings for each week's worship. The Revised Common Lectionary of the Anglican church is one of the most widely used. Judaism uses a similar schedule of scripture called the *parsha, parashah,* or "Torah portion."

- Use focusing tools like counting your breath or the Jesus Prayer as needed.

External Focus (3-5 minutes)

- **Read the day's entry in your chosen devotional.** *For today's purpose, use the reflection I've provided below.*

- **Note:** If you later decide to use this template and choose a daily devotional to use, you'll likely need to make the following adjustment. Many daily devotionals end with a prompting question for reflection or prayer. To translate that devotional prompt into our four-part process, you'll likely skip their provided questions and instead respond using the following two questions:

  - **First, what does this scripture or devotional entry suggest about your inner life?** Where do I see this prompt intersecting with my current experience? (Inward Reflection)

  - **Second, what does this scripture or devotional entry tell you about God and God's character?** How does this aspect of God's character speak to my situation? (Godward Reflection)

Today's Devotional Entry

"For we are his workmanship, created in Christ Jesus for good works, which God prepared ahead of time for us to do."[*]

Identity is a big deal these days. There are so many factors we use to define ourselves, so many flags we wave —nationality, ethnicity, religion, gender, sexuality, political party, theological tradition, generational cohort, Myers-Briggs Type, Enneagram Number, and others. The list seems never-ending. In some ways, these identifying

---

factors are necessary, even helpful, as we make sense of who we are in community and relationship. But in other ways the pressure to identify causes such alienation and anxiety.

In the opening of the New Testament book of Ephesians, the Apostle Paul lays out a vision of salvation. We often think of salvation as a rescue. We are saved *from* something. Yet, in this passage, Paul takes another angle, focusing instead on what we are saved *for*.

"We are His workmanship . . ." the verse begins. The Greek word translated as "workmanship" is *poema*. This is where we get our English word "poem." It speaks of something handmade, crafted with artisanal care. It also evokes creativity. Poems and paintings aren't just made by hand; they are a manifestation of the heart and intention of their artist. Every work of art contains the character and vision of its creator.

The Apostle suggests that you are, in your deepest identity, a work of God's creativity, imbued with some aspect of God's vision and nature. You are not, however, art made to sit on a shelf.

The verse continues, ". . . created in Christ Jesus for good works which God prepared ahead of time . . ." You and I have purpose. We are part of God's good work in the world. The Greek word translated as "good" is *agathos*, which also means "beautiful." Think about that! You, in your essential identity, are an expression of God's creativity. You are good and beautiful and are intended to bring good and beautiful things into the world.

Part of the story of salvation is what we are saved from, but it may be more important to spend time reflecting on what God has saved us for. This passage suggests we get to be part of God's good and beautiful work in the world, expressing God's character of love in our words and actions. That central and divinely ordained identity ought to inform every other identity label we wear, shaping what we do and say in the world.

Inward Reflection (10 minutes)

- Set timer for 10 minutes.

- Copy the scripture at the top of the devotional above into your journal.

- **Reflect on how this devotional reading intersects with your life. Use any of the following questions to get the ball rolling:**

  - *In what ways do you find this verse or commentary personally encouraging?*

  - *In what ways, if any, do you feel resistance to what this verse is suggesting? Why?*

  - *How might life be different if you thought of yourself as an expression of God's character intended to bring good and beautiful things into the world?*

Godward Reflection (8 minutes)

- Set timer for 8 minutes.

- **Reflect on what this verse suggests about the character of God.** Use any of the following questions to get started.

  - *How would you describe the God this verse portrays?*

  - *How might considering God as an artistic creator, like a poet or painter, impact how you see yourself and God's work in your life?*

  - *If God is an artist who gave you the purpose of bringing good and beautiful things into the world, what might God say today about the pressing matters in your life?*

Prayer (5 minutes)

- **Sit in silence** for a timed 1 minute.
  - Pay attention to any inward sense of direction.
- **End by writing a closing prayer.**
  - Write a sentence of prayer for the main people in your life.
  - Pray over your agenda for the day.
  - Ask God for guidance and commit yourself to that guidance.

Week 4, Day 4
The 50-Minute Inner Life Reflection

Introduction

One reason journaling is so effective as a spiritual practice is that it slows us down. Lean into that slowness if your life allows the space. It's possible to approach a shorter journaling session without rush, but a longer block with more margin offers great benefit. Forty-five to seventy-five minutes provides the space to settle into the deep places of your inner life. Today's template is fifty minutes long, so you can get a feel for the extended experience.

This template is also an example of how your journal can focus on a particular area of spiritual or personal growth. For several years, I used this very template. I was in therapy dealing with the consequences of decades of emotional disconnectedness. While my journaling remained spiritually focused, it incorporated elements that dove-tailed with my emotional healing process. My focus on emotions might not be what you need, but this will show you how you can bring a spiritual focus to any area of growth.

This template also includes a passage of scripture as the outside prompt.* Most Christians are familiar with reading scripture devotionally, which is a natural fit for this process. If you want to include scripture, it's best to have a passage

---

* Quick note for you if you're not Christian or if the Bible has been a source of pain in your life: The key in this template is to have a predetermined source of inspirational material that can be taken in small segments. I've worked with people who have used other materials as their "devotional text." This might include poetry or other spiritual readings. There are several examples in Appendix 4: Ways to Practice. For the purpose of this test run, it will be simplest if you can use the text I've provided, but if the Bible is presently a no-go space for you, I understand. Select something short with depth. The process will still work because you're here with the intention to grow and the Spirit is already at work in you.

predetermined; otherwise, you'll waste time hunting for one.* An easy way to predetermine your scripture is to read sequentially through a book or section of the Bible. When I was using this template, I was reading through the Gospel of John a few verses at a time.

For today, you can use the scripture I've provided below unless you're currently using a sequential reading plan of some kind and want to use the next passage in that.

The 50-Minute Inner Life Reflection

- Gather your tools and settle.
- A Bible or Bible-reading app, unless you're using some other material as a prompt.
- Set your timer in each section of this template.

Silence (3 minutes)

- **Sit in silence** for a timed 3 minutes.
- Use focusing tools as needed.

Catching Up With Yourself (12 minutes)

- **Highs & Lows**
  - *List your "high point" and "low point" since your last journal entry. Briefly note why each experience was a high or low.*
- **Emotional Inventory**
  - *Do an emotional inventory. Articulate how you are feeling presently and why.*
  - Note conflicting emotions. Pay attention to the different sensations in your body (e.g. areas of tightness, places of soreness, pain, heat or cold; these sensations are often tied to different body

---

* Don't even get me started on the practice of randomly flipping to a verse to see what God wants to say to you. The distinction between this and divination is a hair's-breadth of self-justification. Whether you're poking entrails or Bible-verses, you're expecting God to perform on command, and that's not how God works.

states that correspond with our different emotions.) Note if the emotions are immediate (reflecting something you're feeling right now) or whether they are echoes (reflecting emotional responses to something that happened since you journaled last.)

Today's Prompt for Reflection (10 minutes)

- **Read & Reflect**
  - **Open to your predetermined scripture or other chosen prompt.** T*oday, use John 3:1-8.*
  - **Write the verse citation in your journal.** Write just the address, "John 3:1-8," not the whole passage. This serves as a reference in case you look back on this entry later. If you're using other material as your prompt, note a page number so you can find the section later if you need to.
  - **As you read the passage, briefly jot your thoughts, reflections, or questions.**
  - This isn't meant to be in-depth study. Just be inquisitive.

Inward Reflection (10 minutes)

- **In your journal, let the selected prompt speak to your inner life using these questions:**
  - *Having read the scripture or prompt, scan back through your "Highs and Lows" and your Emotional Inventory. Note any connecting points between these aspects of your inner life and what you read.*
    - *How might these words speak into your current situation and experience?*
    - *What is your emotional response to these words?*
    - *Why do you think that is?*

Godward Reflection (10 minutes)

- **Reflect on what the prompt suggests about the character of God.** Use any of the following questions to get started.

  - *What, if anything, do these words seem to say about the character of God?*

  - *If this image of God is encouraging to you, why do you think that is?*

  - *If this image of God is hard or raises difficult questions, why do you think that is?*

Prayer (5 minutes)

- **Sit in silence** for a timed 1 minute.

  - Pay attention to any inward sense of direction.

- **Bullet-point out any situations, issues, or people that have surfaced during your journaling,** bringing them into God's presence.

  - Write your prayer for that entry.

  - If you have no specific prayer request for that entry, simply write "Have mercy," "Blessings," or some other simple prayer of intention.

- As a **prayer of gratitude,** take a moment to list several things you can quickly think of (particularly since you last journaled) that you are grateful for.

- **End by writing a closing prayer.**

  - Ask God for guidance and commit yourself to that guidance.

Don't Customize Just Yet!

Read & Reflect

Now you've tried four different templates for journaling—those you experienced over the last three days and the simple template you used last week. You've also repeatedly heard how easy it is to customize the journaling template for your season of life and needs. Before you rush off to design the perfect template, pause a moment.

The best next step is to pick one of these four templates and use it without making any changes. Do this for *at least* a couple of weeks. For the best outcome, use the example template for six weeks. Why? Because you're here to build a habit! Habits take hold through repetition. In the early days of a habit, it's best to make very few changes, and then only necessary ones.

There's another reason. You're just beginning to get familiar with the spine of the process. Customizing the template will introduce other elements and with them possible side-tracks and detours. Until you've built experience with the spine, customization can be a distraction.

Of the options you've tried so far, I recommend most people start with the **30-minute Guided Devotional** (pg. 79). It's a manageable block of time. It uses a daily devotional book as the prompt, which means you don't need to worry about finding a particular focus or scripture. Just select a devotional book (I recommend several in Appendix 4: Ways to Practice) and let that set your direction for a few weeks.

Get into the groove before you start tweaking things. It's not uncommon to get frustrated after journaling for a few weeks because it hasn't resulted in dramatic changes or profound experiences. This makes as much sense as getting frustrated because going to the gym for a few weeks hasn't produced great abs. The benefit comes over time. In week 6 we'll talk about knowing when to modify your template.

PRACTICE

From here out, you'll be journaling using the template you've selected. There may be other brief instructions or questions for reflection related to the content of the specific day, but those will be kept short. The main thing? **Do your journaling.**

◆ **Select a Template and Get Started**

- **Consider the amount of time you're able to give to journaling right now, and then select one of these three templates.**
  - **The 15-Min Slow Down** (Pg. 77)
  - **The 30-Min Guided Devotional** (Pg. 79)
  - **The 50-Min Inner Life Reflection** (Pg. 85)
- **Use this template today and for the next few weeks.**
- **At the very least, commit to two weeks (or 10 sessions).** For the best outcome, commit to six weeks (or 30 sessions). Decide on how many weeks you're going to commit to and write this commitment in your journal.

◆ **Reflect briefly on your commitment to try this process.** Use any of these prompts:

- **How does the idea of committing to a template for several weeks hit you? Why?**
- **What benefit do you think is likely if you use a template for the next 2-6 weeks?**

Week 5

Empowering Your Habit

You're starting the first full week of using the template you've chosen for your journaling practice. You know everything you need to know to do this practice on a day-to-day basis.

Now we'll look toward the future. For journaling to become a regular and sustainable part of your life, it needs to become a habit. Bad habits seem to bloom spontaneously, but most good ones don't. Building a new habit takes attention and care. This week and next, we'll focus on how you can make this habit-building process easier and more successful. Habit building isn't a mystery. There are several key functions of your brain that allow habits to take root. If you understand these, you can use them for your benefit.

This week continue to journal using the template you've chosen. As you do, I'll share several principles for building lasting habits for your reflection.

NOTICE COMPETING HABITS

READ & REFLECT

Your entire life is made of habits. This is one of the most crucial things to keep in mind while building a new habit.

Perhaps your morning is rushed because it's your habit to sleeping in as long as possible. Maybe your evenings pass quickly because it's just so easy to stream the next video. The habit of checking social media whenever you have more than 30 seconds of downtime can make it seem like you never really get a break.

This new habit of journaling is fragile. Good intentions are insufficient. Scheduling a journal session on your calendar isn't enough. The habits you already have are stronger than the habit you're trying to build. Give your new habit the best chance of taking root by noticing where competing habits stand in the way.

One person I worked with decided to journal daily after taking their kids to school. This seemed an ideal time slot. As the weeks passed, though, they were erratic with their new practice. In order to understand this inconsistency, we looked at what else was happening around the time they had set aside for journaling.

It turned out this person had a habit of cleaning the kitchen after getting home from the morning route. They just couldn't ignore the dirty sink and messy counters. The internal pressure of this habit trumped their good intention. They'd say to themselves, "This will only take a moment." Very often, though, the cleaning led to putting something away which led to another project. Without even noticing, the time allotted for journaling had evaporated, and the pressure of daily obligation meant another day skipped.

For this person, seeing the messy counters was a trigger that anchored their cleaning habit. Since every rushed morning included making breakfast and lunch for the kids, the kitchen was always messy when they returned and the trigger fired. This person didn't even know they were acting out a habitual script that overpowered their desire to journal.

You may not feel this way about a dirty kitchen, but you have other triggers in your life that launch deeply ingrained habits. Think about the time and place you've set aside for journaling. Pay close attention to any habits that make keeping that commitment difficult. When you notice competing habits, decide which is more important for who you want to be. If both are important, think about what small changes might allow these habits to coexist.

For example, when this person noticed their habitual pattern, they articulated that a deeper spiritual life was more important to them than a spotless kitchen. They still wanted a clean kitchen but decided to set a 15-minute timer for focused cleaning. This reset the space and allowed them to feel at peace. When the timer went off, the cleaning ended. This prevented rabbit-trailing into new projects. Then they sat down to journal before moving on with their day. This small change cleared space so the new habit of journaling could take hold.

PRACTICE

◆ **Journal**

- **Continue with your selected template.** Add this brief reflection:

◆ **Reflect briefly on today's discussion of competing habits.** Use any of these prompts:

- **Think about the timeframe you've chosen for journaling. Do you notice any preexisting habits that might impact your ability to show up regularly in the necessary space, time, and mindset?**

- **If so, can these competing habits coexist? What changes would allow for that?**

- **If they can't coexist, what changes are you prepared to make?**

ANCHOR A CHAIN TRIGGER

READ & REFLECT

Yesterday I told you about someone who intended to build a habit of daily journaling. They made a reasonable decision about a time and place. They had a firm intention and a plan. Even so, the new habit didn't stick at first because a competing habit was already in place.

The competing habit had two things all habits require: a trigger and a reward. The trigger was powerful because it was tangible (a messy kitchen!) and built into their typical daily schedule (taking the kids to school). A lifetime of being told that responsible people clean up after themselves provided an additional psychological hook. This trigger could not be ignored!

The reward was also immediate and compelling. For this person, a clean kitchen was a small victory over chaos. The deep-breath satisfaction of feeling responsible felt like success. This wouldn't be a reward for everyone, but for this person it was like candy!

This cycle of trigger and reward is the mechanism that builds habits—good or bad. Maybe I habitually eat ice cream before bed and I want to stop. The trigger is the feeling of being drained at the end of a long day. "Ahh... I'm so worn out. Wouldn't a treat be nice?" Ice cream, of course, is fantastic. Not only does it taste great, but it also provides a release of dopamine and a burst of energy. After doing this a few times, my brain links the trigger (being tired at the end of a long day) to the reward (delicious taste and dopamine). The more natural and frequent the trigger, and the more compelling the reward, the stronger the habit becomes.

To change any habit, you have to interrupt this cycle. You can remove the trigger, or you can dislodge the reward. To be successful, you usually need some combination of both. Building a new habit becomes much easier when you understand the trigger/reward cycle.

First, be intentional about your trigger. A commitment to "journal more," or even to "journal five days a week," sounds good, but the goal is too abstract. It's not rooted in the conditions of your life. You're hoping good intentions or memory will provide the trigger. For most of us this is simply insufficient.

It's far better to set a goal that is attached to a realistic trigger. For example, instead of committing to "journal five days a week," commit to "journal five days a week, immediately after breakfast." This goal anchors your new habit to something that's already on the schedule, something you're likely going to do every day. This is called a chain trigger. You are chaining your new habit to a trigger that's already part of your life. A good chain trigger is something that recurs regularly. This leverages your schedule and already existing habits to make it easier for you to remember the new habit and follow through on it.

The goal to "journal five days a week" is really just stating an ideal. "If everything works out, I'd ideally like to journal five days a week." (Yeah, me too!) An ambiguous goal like this floats away in the fast currents of life. Notice how this same goal sounds different when framed with the trigger as a "When/I Will" commitment: "When I get home from taking the kids to school, I will journal." There's a specific time and a concrete sequence of actions. There's an internal motion that leads naturally into the new habit. Also, notice this: The idea of journaling five days a week is not even mentioned, yet because school happens five days a week, that goal is likely to be met without even thinking about it. That's the power of a chain trigger!

Take note of the tangible nature of these commitments and the clear sense of motion built into each:

- **"When I eat lunch at work, I will take thirty minutes to journal."**

- **"When my thirty-minutes-to-bedtime alarm goes off on my phone, I will journal."**

- **"When I lock up the store at closing before heading home, I will sit down to journal for thirty minutes."**

Each of these examples anchors the new habit by chaining it to a sequence of events that is likely to occur naturally. The typical course of life pulls the trigger without any extra effort.

PRACTICE

◆ **Journal**

- **Continue with your selected template,** and add this brief reflection:

◆ **Reflect briefly on the idea of anchoring your new habit with a Chain Trigger.**

- **What habits or patterns already exist in your life, in or around your preferred time to journal, that you can anchor your journaling habit to?**

- **How would you state your journaling goal in a way that includes the trigger?**

Week 5, Day 3
Choose An Effective Reward

Read & Reflect

All habits—good and bad—are built through the cycle of recurring triggers and rewards. Today, we turn our attention to the reward.

Certainly you've heard of using rewards to motivate yourself to do hard things. Finish a tough project, then treat yourself to a meal at an expensive restaurant. Pay off a debt and celebrate with a long weekend away. It seems intuitive that if you promise yourself something nice, you'll be more likely to do the hard thing. The trouble is that this kind of reward system doesn't work for many people. Why? Because it depends on delayed gratification. Delayed gratification is an important skill. It may be the defining skill of adulthood. Sadly, though, it's the opposite of what's needed to build a habit.

Think about how bad habits form so easily. Rarely is the reward some distant, imagined benefit. There's no delay because gratification is baked into the habit itself. The more immediate the reward and more directly it's tied to the action, the more quickly the habit forms. Destructive habits usually have immediate intrinsic rewards. Healthy habits often don't. Most people don't get a dopamine rush walking into the gym, at least not at first. Building a habit of journaling is similar. Except for those few who deeply love writing, many can quickly come to feel like journaling is a chore.

If you already know that a large delayed reward works for you, by all means, use it. Most people, however, need something more immediate. Think about the different aspects of the habit you want to build and how you might include something pleasant in the process.

Could the location be the reward? You might create a peaceful and enjoyable corner in your home for journaling. You might select a nearby coffee shop that has great pastries. Could the tools be part of the reward? Using a beautiful journal and high-quality pen is part of the fun for some. If you are a coffee or tea lover, brewing a fresh cup to accompany your journaling might add enjoyment. If you're an introvert, having a built-in block of solitary quiet might be a reward in itself.

What if those ideas don't seem fun at all? Likely, journaling is not something you'd choose to do for enjoyment. Maybe you'd rather be doing something active or with people. In that case, you can structure your time so that the reward happens immediately after journaling is done. If you love running, take your morning run as soon as you finish journaling. Or perhaps that's when you make a phone call to a friend to chat.

Building and maintaining a habit is much easier when the entire trigger-reward chain is in place. Think through your life and consider how you can set yourself up for the easiest process of habit building.

First, identify a trigger. The ideal trigger occurs naturally and regularly in your life. You don't have to remember to do the habit because the trigger automatically brings it to mind. Second, ensure the resources necessary for the habit are immediately available. In the case of journaling, the resources are the space and the tools—your pen and journal, your laptop, a cleared kitchen table, the nearby coffee shop. You don't have to dig these things up or decide which to use. They are already selected and available. Third, see that the process leads directly to a reward that's either built into the process or happens immediately following.

Your sequence should be **Trigger > Journal > Reward**. The more consistently this sequence happens, the more quickly and easily your habit will take root. The more the reward is integrated into your practice, the stronger its motivating power. All your bad habits were built with this very mechanism; you just didn't notice it was happening! Good habits can be built in the same way.

PRACTICE

◆ **Journal.**

- **Continue with your selected template,** and add this brief reflection:

◆ **Reflect briefly on how you might use rewards to strengthen your new habit of journaling.**

- **Considering the examples shared above, what kinds of rewards might you be able to incorporate into your journaling practice?**

NOTICE & NAME YOUR WINS

READ & REFLECT

There is another kind of reward you can add to your experience. This one's not automatic and immediate like the rewards we discussed yesterday. It requires a bit of attention and practice, but it can build your positive attitude toward journaling. This reward? Noticing and naming small wins.

Habits are easier to build when there is a clear benefit. Your brain's wiring reinforces this. When you experience a clear benefit, your brain releases those good chemicals that create a sense of satisfaction, but the benefit from something like journaling is often abstract, at least for a while. The idea of investing in spiritual growth just doesn't trigger dopamine release for most people. So, another way you can intentionally build positive association is to consciously take a moment just after journaling to reflect and notice the wins.

The win might be something obvious. Maybe as you journaled, you felt a deep sense of peace or God's presence. That's not likely to happen every day, but when it happens, notice it and be grateful for it. Explicitly express that gratitude: "I'm grateful I felt peace today while I journaled." "I'm grateful that today I sensed I was not alone." Breathe deeply. Say those words out loud. Write them at the end of your journal entry.

Most days your journaling isn't going to feel transcendent, but even the routine days hold small wins if you look. Maybe you learned something about a scripture passage. Perhaps you saw one of your relationships more clearly. You might have completed a full week of journaling. Or maybe the only win you can see is that you successfully resisted the pressure to rush for 15 minutes. That matters! Close your journaling session by taking a moment to notice and name the wins, especially the smallest ones, with gratitude.   Each time you do this, you're building positive associations with journaling. You're also training yourself to look for the wins, even training yourself to be more conscious of God's presence. We're more likely to notice what we're looking for.

Naming your wins will be especially important if you don't enjoy writing or if spiritual practices like this are new for you. You need to notice and name tangible wins as you go. Do this regularly, and you'll quickly build a web of positive memories and experiences associated with your journaling practice.

PRACTICE

◆ **Journal.**

- **Continue with your selected template,** and add this brief reflection:

◆ **Reflect briefly on how noticing the small wins can help you build this habit.**

- **What small wins did you notice in your journaling time today?** Name at least one and express gratitude for it.

- **Why might this practice of noticing and naming small wins help your habit-building and spiritual journey?**

LIVE IN PRACTICAL GRACE

READ & REFLECT

Life presents so many obstacles to thoughtful reflection. Habits that contribute to spiritual growth are difficult to build. Our competing commitments hinder us. Unexpected circumstances throw our good intentions into disarray. Our many obligations squeeze our margins of time and energy. There is, however, an obstacle greater than all of these. This impediment is not something life throws at us; it's something we do. Or rather, something we don't do. Many of us don't have grace for ourselves.

A new habit is, by definition, something we haven't mastered. We're going to do it poorly. We're going to forget things. When we miss a few days, it breaks our streak. This can feel demoralizing. For a perfectionist this deficiency feels very close to failure. We naturally distance ourselves from what doesn't feel good. We say things like, "Maybe it's not the right time," or "Maybe this practice just doesn't work for me." These justifications feel better than facing the discomfort of not doing something well. Even those of us who are not perfectionists can feel the weight of this internal judgment. Self-condemnation kills new habits.

Keep this in mind: the only safe environment for a pursuit of spiritual growth is grace.* You aren't earning something. You're not putting on a show or accomplishing something for credit. The only worthwhile purpose for your growth endeavor is to become more present to yourself and God. God knows you're imperfect. God isn't measuring your spiritual practice against other people. You will miss days. Life will happen. Your good intentions will wear thin. Any guilt or shame you feel is an

---

* Cindy Brosh, a therapist who consulted on this book, commented: "Neurologically speaking, it's difficult to stay regulated when experiencing shame. Extending grace and non-judgement to ourselves keeps us out of our midbrain (the part most dedicated to survival) and allows us to hold that multiple things can be true at once."

unnecessary emotional weight you're piling on top of the experience.

Without shame or judgment, simply start again tomorrow. God knows your circumstances, your obligations, and the intentions of your heart. Yes, keeping a commitment is important. Sure, consistency is the fastest path to a new habit. Yet, rigid commitment to those good things can set you up for failure.

Here's an example: At one point, I had decided to get up at 6 AM, wake up the kids so they could get ready for school, and then do my journaling. My kids were eight and nine at the time. (You can already see where this is heading, I'm sure.) My plan was a disaster. I was frustrated with my kids because they couldn't get ready on their own. I was frustrated with myself because I couldn't keep my commitment to journal. Each morning was a rushed power struggle that left the kids and I feeling grumpy.

The problem wasn't my kids. It wasn't realistic to expect my kids to get themselves ready for school without my help. As soon as I decided to journal after the kids left for school, not only was it easier to keep my commitment, but my attitude with the kids improved dramatically.

Practical grace allows us to redefine our commitment when we've set ourselves up poorly. Grace allows us to make room for unforeseen circumstances. It gives us permission to flex when we just don't have the emotional energy. It means we don't shift into blame or condemnation (or if we do, we notice, smile, and try again). God's heart toward you is an endless well of grace. Practice relating to yourself in the same way.

PRACTICE

◆ **Journal.**

- **Continue with your selected template,** and add this brief reflection:

◆ **Reflect briefly on the role of practical grace in your spiritual growth.**

- **Do you consider yourself a perfectionist? Why or why not? Do you have any character tendencies that might make it hard for you to stick with this habit? What are they?**

- **How can you embody practical grace for yourself as you build the habit?**

- **How might practical grace serve you in other parts of your life?**

WEEK 6
ONGOING MAINTENANCE

Aristotle is credited with saying, "We are what we repeatedly do. Excellence then is not an act, but a habit."[*] Spiritual growth, similarly so. We can pray, read scripture, participate in a faith community, and many other religious activities.[†] None of these actions bear fruit if we do them once. Only through faithfulness over time will our spiritual practices do their work in us.[‡]

What we do regularly and repeatedly shape us. We live in a grasping, fearful, self-centered society. The routine of surviving this world forms us in its image. Unless we resist, we will become more self-centered, more brittle, wrapped up in our security, position, or sense of control. One way we resist this pressure is to build spiritual practices into our lives. These practices, if we are faithful to them, enable us to keep a clear head and soft heart.

Journaling is one such habit. If you stick with it over the long term, you will find you are a better person for it. This final week together, we'll talk about ways you can keep this habit fresh so that it remains a part of your life for years to come.

---

[*] Historian Will Durant is the actual author of these words. In *The Story of Philosophy*, he quotes Aristotle, from *Nicomachean Ethics*: "These virtues are formed in man by his doing the actions." Following that quote, Durant summarizes Aristotle with the now famous phrase. Will Durant, "VII. Ethics and the Nature of Happiness," in *The Story of Philosophy: The Lives and Opinions of the Great Philosophers of the Western World* (New York, NY: Simon and Schuster, 2009), p. 98.

[†] Insert practices from any other tradition, and the point remains the same.

[‡] Eugene Peterson aptly described this as "a long obedience in the same direction."

Week 6, Day 1
Be Realistic About the Time Needed

Read & Reflect

If you're following the steps, then you've just finished the second week of journaling using a template. I suspect you've already noticed that this process of building a journaling habit will extend beyond the end of this little book. Unrealistic expectations create frustration. So, let's talk about a realistic time frame for building a habit like this.

If you are journaling frequently (by that, I mean more than four days a week), here's what you can expect.* For the first four to six weeks, you're trying something new. It will feel interesting just because it's novel. It may feel validating because you're doing something tangible for your spiritual growth. But this isn't a habit yet; it's a test drive. It will feel awkward and hard.

After six to ten weeks, the habit will begin to take root. If you've anchored journaling to a strong trigger, you won't need to remind yourself to do it anymore. Once that automatic process kicks in, you have a habit. That's worth celebrating! Keep in mind, though, that this new habit is fragile.

After about ten weeks of regular practice, your new habit will become an automatic part of your routine. The practice itself won't feel new anymore. You're no longer sorting out how to do it. You've ironed out issues with your tools or space. The template you use feels second nature. You may even begin to notice your body physically relax as you sit down to journal.

Somewhere between three to six months is when your mind and heart will fully settle into the habit. This is when you'll start to notice a consistently positive impact on your life. Unexpected circumstances will still interrupt, but you may find you miss the practice on the days you can't do it. When you come back after missing days, sitting down to journal will feel like coming home.

---

* This habituation process will take longer if you're journaling less frequently. If you're very inconsistent, it may never happen. On the other hand, if you're already comfortable with contemplative practices, or other modes of journaling, the process may go much more quickly for you.

This means you have built a stable, durable, and meaningful habit.

Ideally, you won't start tweaking your template until six weeks into your practice, or at least until the trigger becomes automatic. Even then, don't make significant changes to the process until you're settled enough to feel "at home" with the practice. That usually happens after three to six months, and then you can safely make changes to your template. Even so, when you make changes, always keep some aspect of your practice consistent. Too many changes all at once can disrupt the habit entirely.

No matter where you are in the process, you will have days when you don't feel like doing it. You will have days when it doesn't feel good, and you wonder if it makes any difference. These are the days when you bring to mind your larger goal. You began this endeavor to know yourself better and more consistently connect with God's Spirit. The hard days, the days that don't feel meaningful, are the days when you are building the muscle of faithfulness. Showing up matters.

PRACTICE

◆ **Journal.**

- **Continue with your selected template,** and add this brief reflection:

◆ **Reflect briefly on the timeline presented today.**

- **Where do you see yourself in this habit-building timeline?**

- **What has been challenging so far about building this journaling habit? What has been meaningful or helpful?**

WEEK 6, DAY 2

MAKE WISE CHANGES

READ & REFLECT

After you've established your habit of journaling, you'll find it's quite adaptable. Making changes to keep the process fresh and valuable is part of what makes this a life-long habit, but it's important to make changes wisely.

Small Changes

From time to time you may need to make small changes to adapt the practice to your life and needs. A change in schedule might mean you need to bump your whole routine back 15 minutes. If your template uses a daily devotional for the prompt, you'll need to pick something new when you come to the end of what you're using. Perhaps you'll find yourself struggling with cynicism so you add a daily gratitude list to help with your state of mind.

These simple changes usually only involve one aspect of your routine and can be implemented without causing upheaval. As long as you're not making these kinds of small changes weekly, make them when you need to.

Seasonal Changes

Sometimes it makes sense to change many parts of your journaling habit all at once. This usually happens when you have a significant change in your life or find yourself moving into a new season. Because your journaling is helping you mature spiritually, your practice needs to adapt to the season of life and growth you're in.

One of the significant seasonal changes for me was when I finished a several-year-long run of therapy. The next step was for me to practice what I'd learned on my own. My journal had been an integral part of the therapy process with a significant focus on my emotional life. Now that I was moving on from therapy, the emotional aspect would still matter, but it would no longer be primary.

Using just the four core elements, I spent several days journaling about where I was at personally, emotionally, and spiritually. I decided I wanted to learn more about spiritual discernment. That led me to incorporate elements of the classic Ignatian Examen in my journaling.* This ancient prayer method includes several sections that replaced some of the template structure I'd been using. Because the new direction made significant changes to my habit, I decided to keep the same time and place to provide consistency.

Periodic Review

I've also found that periodically reviewing my process ensures that what I'm doing is still aligned with my larger goals. I've settled into doing this review every fall. I presently have school-aged kids, and my wife is a teacher, so the fall is a natural time for new expectations and changing schedules. So, even the timing of the review is based on my current life season.

During this review, I look at every element. I look at the logistical aspects like where I'm journaling, when, how often and how long. I also look at each part of my template to ensure all four spine elements are represented in a way that works for where I'm at. I pay attention to my current sense of where I'd like to grow. One year an area of growth I wanted to focus on was my relationship with my daughter. As part of this, I decided to pray for her and for how I could support her. Of course, I'd prayed for her in the past, but this particular year, I committed to praying for our relationship every day. Another year, because I started graduate school, I knew I would be carrying a heavy load of reading and writing, so it made sense to scale my journaling practice back to something simpler.

It may also be worthwhile to scan back through your journaling of the past season. You may notice themes developing.

---

*The Ignatian Examen, also called the Daily Examen, is a form of prayer taught by Ignatius of Loyola, a 15th century Catholic priest and theologian. This method of prayer was designed to help people practice spiritual discernment in their daily lives. You can learn more about this practice in the Resources section of Appendix 4: Ways to Practice.

You may see ways you've grown that you hadn't noticed. One reader even mentioned that it was in scanning back over her journal content that she was able to identify that she had Seasonal Affective Disorder. Seeing the change in tone and prayer over the year made this visible for her.

A periodic review provides a natural time for discontinuing elements that are no longer helpful, which keeps the practice both fresh and sustainable over the long haul. Because I know I'm going to do this review regularly, I'm more willing to give new elements a good try. When it comes time for a review like this, you'll find a guide in the Appendix 2: Building and Evaluating Your Journal Template.

When you make any changes big or small, keep the **Trigger > Journal > Reward** sequence in mind. If you find that your trigger stops working automatically, that means something needs addressing. Your life's routine may have changed enough that you need a new trigger to anchor your habit to. Or you may need to focus again on faithfulness and consistency. As long as this cycle is working, make whatever small changes necessary to keep the process relevant and working for you.

PRACTICE

◆ **Journal.**

- **Continue with your selected template,** and add this brief reflection:

◆ **Reflect briefly on making changes to your template.**

- You'll always need to balance the tension between two factors: 1) Maintaining consistency to support a strong habit, and 2) Making necessary changes to keep the practice relevant to your needs.

- **Think about your personality and how you relate to change. Do you think you need the process to be more consistent or more flexible for you to be able to stick with it over time? Why?**

- **Does it seem helpful to have some periodic review? How frequent makes sense for you? Quarterly? Annually? Something else?** Write your plan in your journal. If you use a planner or reminder app, schedule the next review at the appropriate time.

WEEK 6, DAY 3

IMPLEMENT A FTF ROUTINE

READ & REFLECT

Today I'd like to share an additional practice that can augment your journaling habit. Perhaps you'll find it helpful.

After many years of experimentation, I've learned that I get the most tangible benefit from my journaling practice if I do it first thing in the morning. There have been seasons where it made more sense to do it at another time, but I keep returning to morning journaling because it seems to make more of a difference for me. I suspect the impact is greater because I'm setting the tone for my whole day. I seem to be more flexible and gracious when I start with reflection and attention to my inner world and God's presence.

In addition to journaling in the morning, I have added other elements to my morning ritual. I call this my First Things First (FTF) routine.* "First Things First" is a saying from the recovery world. To the addict it's both a reminder and a warning. If you don't attend to the things that matter first, you put your recovery in jeopardy. This is wisdom for all of us.

We all have important priorities, but the rushed pace of life means many of us don't invest time in these things. Without that regular engagement, our priorities fade into aspirational ideals. An FTF routine is a daily practice that keeps your priorities central, no matter what your day brings you.

---

* Earlier in this book, I said you could journal anytime during the day that works for you. I said that morning is no more spiritual than evening. All true. If you've discovered by now that journaling in the evening works best for you, fantastic. Stick with what's working. The point of the FTF routine is not necessarily to journal in the morning. The point is to start your day in a way that aligns with your ideals and goals. So, even if you are a night person, you have a "first moment" each day. I'm going to advocate that for your spiritual health and maturity, you make use of your "first moment" *whenever it comes*, to set the tone for your day. Even if you find that journaling works best for you in the evening, you can still do something intentional and simple with a FTF practice that will set you up for a better day.

An FTF routine sequences several activities you've chosen because they reflect your priorities. Not only are you focusing on your spiritual maturity with journaling, but you are taking other tangible steps toward who you want to be.

For several years my FTF routine looked like this:

- **Rolling out of bed at 5:30 AM and into workout clothes that I laid out the night before.**[*]

- **Do the 7-Minute work-out.**[†]

- **Walk on my treadmill at a brisk pace for 30 minutes while listening to a spiritually focused podcast.**

- **Brew a pot of tea.**

- **Read 15 minutes in a book that has spiritual or theological insight.**

- **Read 15 minutes in a book about personal or professional development.**

- **Do my journaling. I was using the emotion-focused template that I shared with you in Week 4.**

- **Close with prayer and start my day.**

This routine took about two hours total. With this daily process, I was investing in several aspects of my life that matter to me: physical health, spiritual health, professional development, and emotional recovery. At other times, my FTF has been much shorter and less involved. If you choose to implement an FTF routine, the activities you include should reflect your priorities, not mine. Many of us have lives where much of the day we have to be reactive to others, serving agendas that aren't our own. A FTF routine means that before you start down that roller coaster, you have already invested in what matters most to you. A FTF routine can improve your life and strengthen your journaling.

---

[*] Laying out my workout clothes the night before is an example of a habit trigger. In the morning, the workout clothes are immediately available. No thinking is required. Putting them on is an automatic reaction to waking up that starts the sequence of the entire FTF routine, and all before my conscious mind is really able to put up a fight.

[†] Learn more about this quick work-out routine backed by solid science at this website: https://live210.com/seven-min-workout/

You declare ownership

When you start your day with a FTF routine, you are saying, "I am the steward of my time. Regardless of how I must spend the rest of this day, my time is my own." With this attitude you are less likely to live with a reactive attitude. You are taking responsibility for the most precious gift God has given you. Staking ownership like this becomes a daily declaration of who you will be.

You program your attitude.

A daily FTF routine allows you to place worthy, life-giving thoughts in your mind and heart. The day may come at you with sadness, frustration, anxiety, or other people's pain and fear. You can decide to start your day with your mind "set on things above," that are true, honest, good, noble, and admirable.* Starting with gratitude, spiritual guidance, and other food for your soul will set you up to face whatever comes with more maturity and grace.

You guarantee forward motion.

You have very little control over what comes your way in life. You don't know what situation or crisis will arise. If you start every day with a FTF routine, no matter what happens for the rest of the day, you will have made forward motion. When you slide into bed that night, you'll know you did things that matter, even if the rest of the day was a disappointment or out of your control.

You strengthen your journaling habit

Last week, we talked about how crucial it is to anchor your habit to a strong trigger. Making journaling part of a larger FTF sequence supercharges your trigger. This is called habit-stacking. Habit-stacking is when you chain a series of habits together in such a way that each naturally leads to the next. As each habit grows in strength, the entire sequence grows stronger. One part of the chain may be harder for you or less enjoyable, but because it's embedded in a chain of habits, you're much more likely to stick with it.

---

* See Philippians 4:8.

PRACTICE

◆ **Journal.**

    • **Continue with your selected template.**

◆ **Want to learn more?**

    • **If a FTF routine sounds helpful to you and you'd like to learn more, read this series of short articles:**

        • **Is your Day your Property or Someone Else's?** http://live210.com/ftf1/

        • **The FTF Routine that Gives me Life.** http://live210.com/ftf2/

        • **The Target for a Life-Changing FTF Routine.** http://live210.com/ftf3/

If you'd like more guidance, I teach an online course that includes the FTF routine as one practice for busy people who want a more intentional spiritual life. It's called, **Not Just One More Thing: Spiritual Growth for Busy People**. Learn more about that here: http://live210.com/too-busy.

MAKE LEVEL PATHS

READ & REFLECT

Let your eyes look directly forward
and your gaze be straight before you
Keep straight the path of your feet
and all your ways will be sure.*

These lines from the ancient book of Proverbs offer wisdom for our pursuit. First there's the matter of where we look. Where do we place our attention? If we keep focused on our purpose, we're much more likely to experience forward motion. We're less likely to get lost.

Next we're counseled to keep straight paths. This ancient Hebrew poetry isn't suggesting we walk in a line. It's talking about making the path straight for ourselves. The language conjures imagery of laying a roadway, removing the large rocks and obstacles so that the way forward is smooth and easy. The wisdom offered here is that we can take steps to make our path easier to travel. The opposite is also true.

Think about your journaling habit and all that's involved. Think about what you could do to "keep straight the path." Are there small steps that could make keeping this habit easier? Where do you experience friction? Are there obstacles you can remove? Here are some examples to consider:

If you journal in the morning, one of the best ways to make sure things go well is to mindfully steward the night before. If you stay up too late, if you eat late, if you go to bed on the adrenaline rush of an intense movie, getting up in the morning will be much more challenging. Are there small changed you could make to your night routine that would improve your mornings?

---

* Proverbs 4:25-26, NRSV. Go ahead and read the whole chapter. It's full of good stuff.

If you journal on your computer or a device but find yourself easily distracted by social media, how can you clear away that obstacle? Can you turn off your internet? Can you use a tool like the Freedom App* to turn off those distractions for a while?

Do you find that you have to track down your tools when it's time to journal? Can you gather them in one place and keep them there? If you journal at a coffee shop or other location away from home, can you put your journaling supplies into a small case or shoulder bag, so they are always together and easy to grab on your way out the door?

Think through your routine and notice any points of friction. What can you do to smooth your path? Can you limit any decision-making lag so that your chain of habits can flow automatically? By removing the small obstacles, you are straightening your path to a sustainable practice.†

There are many ways that life and circumstances are simply beyond our control. Gracious flexibility is our best posture for dealing with uncertainty. But there are other ways where we are our own biggest obstacle. In those cases, we can take steps to clear our own path.

---

* Freedom is an online service and app that allows you to turn off your access to social media and other online services when you need to. Learn more about it in the resource list in Appendix 3: Recommended Tools.

† It's possible that your friction point won't be fixed by a small change. Sometimes the obstacle is actually a competing habit with a stronger trigger. Review week 5, day 1 if you think you've uncovered a competing habit.

PRACTICE

◆ **Journal.**

- **Continue with your selected template,** and add this brief reflection:

◆ **Reflect briefly on making your path straight:**

- **In your journal, bullet point out any possible points of friction in your journaling (or FTF) process.**

- **For each friction point, brainstorm possible changes that would make it easier to move past that particular obstacle.**

- **Consider which of these are the easiest to implement or will make the most difference for you. These small decisions make staying faithful to your journaling habit easier over time.**

CHOOSE FAITHFULNESS

READ & REFLECT

You picked up this book because you desire to grow spiritually. You want to mature as a person. Maybe you hope to be more aware of God's presence. Journaling for spiritual growth is one tool to support this desire.

The practice, however, is not as important as the purpose. What matters most is that your heart comes more and more into alignment with God's heart. This isn't something you accomplish with great effort. Don't get tripped up by perfectionism or performance. Don't get lost in the details. Don't judge or shame yourself when things don't go to plan. God is with you in this process. Grace is something to trust, to lean into, to find rest in.

The process I've taught you provides a mirror to see yourself truthfully and trains your inner ear to listen. The physical act of journaling slows you down. In this slower reflective space, you are more able to let go of the masks and agendas that stand in the way of vulnerable intimacy with yourself and God.

At the end of Jesus' ministry, he gathered his closest friends and followers for a final, private meal. He knew his time with them was short. He wanted to leave them guidance that would carry them through the painful and uncertain future. This passage in John's Gospel, often referred to as "the Upper Room discourse," contains some of the most impactful and important spiritual teachings in human history.*

One of the things Jesus said here has the capacity to entirely change the way you experience your life. Jesus was talking to his close friends. For them, following him had been tangible. Where he walked, they walked. When he spoke words, they listened. Their connection to Jesus was concrete, but that was about to

---

* Read the whole thing. John's gospel, chapter 13-17. I suspect there is enough spiritual guidance in these five chapters to serve most of us for our whole lives.

change. With Jesus' upcoming death, following his way would become less concrete and clear. You and I live in that uncertain future Jesus spoke of. His words to his close friends are also for you and me.

Here's what he said: "On that day you will know that I am in my Father, you are in me, and I am in you."* Notice the spiritual geography Jesus describes. He is in the Father. That is a relationship of intimacy and access. In the same way, He is in us, and we are in him. There is no distance, no separation. This is Jesus' radical claim and Divine promise.

The work of spiritual growth is not to build a relationship with God. Jesus taught us that God is already in relationship with humanity and always has been. God's presence isn't something we summon. All spiritual growth is about learning to pay attention.

There is much in our lives that stands in the way of being present. Our busyness and worry, our rush and over-obligation, these and so much else distract and fragment us. This is not how life has to be. Journaling helps us practice being present, paying attention, and listening to our own internal voice and Spirit's guidance. As with any practice, the transformation does not happen overnight, but by grace, it happens as we faithfully learn to listen.

For more than twenty-five years, journaling has been a vital practice in my life. It's become an appointment God regularly uses to challenge, encourage, and shape me. My journal has become a sanctuary where I meet the Spirit and together work through the rough edges of my story. In my journal, I've found hope, correction, courage, and healing. I know how life-changing this practice can be.

So, what's next? If you've set about to build a habit of journaling for spiritual growth, continue in it. You'll miss days. Faithfully return. It won't always feel remarkable or inspiring. Sometimes it will be hard. You may uncover pain in your inner world. Yet, if you stick with it, return to it, holding the practice with gracious flexibility, it will, like a well-tended garden, bear fruit.

---

* John 14:20, CSB.

God is already present in your life working for your spiritual maturity. Journaling is one way you can choose to actively participate in what God is up to. Right now—as we are, without any further effort—we have an intimate, ongoing relationship with God. We are loved. We are known. We are not alone. Practice living in that reality. It will change your life.

PRACTICE

◆ **There is only one thing left. Journal.**

As you do, pay attention, listen, and let God shape your inner world. Blessings on the way!

APPENDIX 1
WHAT IS SPIRITUAL GROWTH?

Few words are quite as squishy as "spiritual," able to be molded by many different people with various intents. Some avoid using it because it's open to so many interpretations. After all, the term is used by all sorts of people, probably even by people who disagree with you! Yet, I think *spiritual* is a worthy and helpful word. Here's why I think so, and how I use it.

We are spiritual beings because God is Spirit,* and we are created in God's image.† Think of spirituality as that which pertains to our essential being. The spiritual life, then, would be the life of the Spirit or perhaps the soul.‡ If this is the domain of Spirit, we might assume things like eternity, heaven, salvation, inner peace, and union with God are most important, but this interior world is not merely religious. Every person has an interior landscape made up of thoughts, emotions, hopes, and expectations. This inner world is molded by experience and contains the stories we hold about ourselves and the world. This is the seedbed of our desires and decisions.

This interior spiritual life is central to who we are, but any view of spirituality that is limited to the realm of ideals, beliefs, or mystical experience ultimately fails because it disregards that we are also physical beings. Our body is not merely a vehicle to

---

* See John 4:24 as one Christian reference point for what this means.

† Genesis 1:27

‡ Some Christian traditions separate "spirit" and "soul" as different, yet both Hebrew and Christian scriptures use their version of these words interchangeably. Sometimes these words simply refer to a person, sometimes they refer to an inner, spiritual part of a person, and other times, particularly with the words translated as "spirit," they refer to other mundane things like wind, breath, or a kind of inner motivation. My own sense of the anthropology found in the Bible is that a human is a whole being integrating both body and spirit. The second Genesis creation poem (Genesis 2) makes this point. God formed a physical body from earth, then breathed into that body the "breath of life," providing a spiritual nature. Only when these two things came together, did the human become "a living being." That English phrase is translated from the Hebrew word *nephesh*, which in other contexts is translated as "soul." A physical body plus a spiritual nature equals a living soul.

move a more essential part of us, like a mind or spirit, around in the world. Our body is a central part of our being. The body and its senses are the only avenue we have with which to experience and relate to the world, others, and even God. So, the spiritual life must also incorporate our embodied life.

One attribute of God's life as Spirit is that God is present everywhere.* An ancient Hebrew poet put it in this way:

> Where can I go from your spirit? Or where can I flee from your presence? If I ascend to heaven, you are there; if I make my bed in Sheol,† you are there . . . If I say, "Surely the darkness shall cover me, and the light around me become night," even the darkness is not dark to you; the night is as bright as the day, for darkness is as light to you.‡

There is no place, no human experience, where God is not present. In contrast, one of the identifying attributes of being human is that we are only bodily present in one place.

The spiritual life, then, comprises the many ways our life intersects with the Spirit of God both in our inner world and in the physical world around us. You could just call all of this *life*, and you wouldn't be wrong. Still, by using the phrase *spiritual life*, we draw attention to our awareness that in all of life—both our inner world and embodied experience—we interact with, experience, and can act in concert with the Spirit of God.

In thinking about this kind of life, I must draw a distinction between religion and spirituality. Religion, at its best, is a container for the spiritual life. This container is made of particular beliefs (doctrines) and practices (rituals) that have emerged within a culture and are transmitted by the participants (community). Religion can sometimes transcend time and culture, but it will always be marked by the effects of time and culture because it is necessarily embodied Things that are embodied must exist in particular times, places, and forms.

---

* 16th century theologians coined the term *omnipresence* to label this attribute of God's existence.

† The Hebrew name for the place of the dead.

‡ Psalm 139:7-12, NRSV.

Religion and spirituality are not the same, but they are inextricably related, like fire and heat. Religion contains and is enlivened by spiritual life. Simultaneously (and I suspect, indivisibly), spiritual life is formed and given expression by religion. So, for example, certain practices can foster spiritual growth, but spiritual growth is not found in the process of becoming more adept at those practices. Participating in a religious community is very nearly an essential part of spiritual growth, yet spiritual growth is far deeper than simply becoming more attached to a religious community. Reading, meditating on, or studying scripture can be a catalyst for Divine encounters, despite the often observed fact that no amount of time spent with scripture can guarantee spiritual growth.

Spiritual growth, then, is that experience of maturing in our essential humanity. We were made in God's image, and God's project with humanity is helping us mature more fully in that image.* We are born necessarily self-centered with a natural desire for survival and self-protection. As we grow, we come to understand that we are not the only beings in the universe and that our life impacts the lives of others. As we mature, if everything is working right, our sense of identity expands to include an ever larger and larger community of those we are willing to sacrifice for. We acknowledge our ego and ego needs while moving away from seeing the world and others as merely objects to serve our ego. In simple terms, we become more loving. Our posture toward the self, the world, and God becomes marked more and more by humble, other-centered, co-suffering, radically inclusive love.†

---

* This is expressed quite clearly by the Apostle Paul in the fourth chapter of Ephesians. This is where Christians found the language of maturing in the image of Christ.

† This phrase represents what I take to be the heart of Jesus' example and teaching. The Christian church as a whole has not always, or even often, aligned with this path, but this is what the best of Christian spirituality offers. This other-centered, co-suffering posture can be found in the lives of countless anonymous Christians and their churches across time and history (as well as in the lives of some famous Christians). These faithful followers of Jesus served others at great cost, walked with those in the margins, and sought to make the world a more just and peaceful place.

This process of growth cannot be forced, but it can be nurtured. The best metaphor I've found is to think of spiritual growth as a garden. The soil is our inner life, what we often simply call, "the heart." The circumstances of our lives, the choices we make, the relationships we build are plants in our garden. What's been planted bears fruit in who we become. The fruit of growing in the life of Spirit is a harvest of character growth, qualities like love, joy, peace, patience, gentleness, and self-control.*

As with a garden, the gardener cannot force growth to happen. Growth naturally occurs. It's the very nature of the organism. Even so, the gardener can tend the soil. They can fertilize and water, remove weeds, and protect from invasive pests and extreme weather. These steps do not make growth happen. They don't "earn" growth through their practice. The fruit that comes is not the result of a transaction.

Spiritual growth, then, comes through our consent to and participation† with the work of the Spirit in us and the world around us. This leads us to mature in the qualities of the Spirit and enables us to embody those qualities in the world. As we mature in our inner life, what is growing in us ripples out into the world around us. We contribute to the forming of communities that reflect these qualities. As we do so, we play a part in God's good and beautiful work in the world. In this way, the spiritual life is not only about us, but simultaneously about how we live in our relationships, and the kind of world we are participating in building.

---

* This list is drawn from the Apostle Paul. He identified these as qualities that would be present in a life that is becoming more Spirit-directed. They are often called "the fruit of the Spirit." See Galatians 5:22-25.

† Dr. Bradley Jersak introduced me to the language of participation and consent as a way to understand how God can be present and involved in the world without overwhelming free will. His book *A More Christlike God* covers this. Find a brief summary here: https://live210.com/jersak-participation-consent/

APPENDIX 2

BUILDING & EVALUATING YOUR JOURNAL TEMPLATE

YOUR FIRST TEMPLATE

These questions can help you set a direction for your new journaling practice and determine your starting template.

- **How much time do you have to spend?**
  - The total amount of time you commit will determine how long each segment should be.
  - There are four core elements: **Silence**, **Inward Reflection**, **Godward Reflection**, and **Prayer**. The Reflection sections should take the largest chunk of time.
  - With shorter sessions (15-20 minutes), you'll only be able to do the four core elements. With more time those elements can expand, and you have space for other things.
- **How are you going to incorporate silence?**
  - Review Week 3, Day 2 for the role silence plays and how to easily incorporate it.
  - For additional ideas, see the resource below in Appendix 4, "Ways to Practice Silence."
- **What areas of self-reflection are the most important for you right now?**
  - Consider your personal and spiritual growth. Are there areas you'd like to focus on or that you sense God might be inviting you to look at?
  - Do you want to use scripture, a daily devotional, or some other reading as the prompt? Did you have something in mind?

- For additional ideas, see the resources below in Appendix 4, "Using Scripture for Reflection," "Using Other Reading For Reflection," and "Recommended Daily devotionals."

- **Note:** If you use a single reading as a prompt, like scripture or a daily devotional, you will respond to that single reading with two different responses. First, you'll use the prompt as a jumping-off point for Inward Reflection. Then, you'll use the same prompt but focus on a Godward Reflection. Review Week 3, Day 3, and 4, for the basics of these two areas of reflection.

- There are other ways to focus your time of self-reflection besides scripture or other readings. For ideas, see Appendix 4, "Additional Options for Inward Reflection."

- **What ways of reflecting on God and God's character are the most helpful in this season of your life?**

  - Considering your needs and areas of growth, are there aspects of God's character that would be helpful for you to focus on?

  - Do you want to use scripture, a daily devotional, or some other reading as the prompt? Did you have something in mind? Remember, this will be the same prompt you used in the Inward Reflection segment.

  - For additional ideas, see Appendix 4, "Additional Options for Godward Reflection."

- **What prayer practices will be part of your journaling?**

  - Remember that your entire journaling practice is a form of prayer if trust God's presence is your starting point.

  - It's a good idea to end your session with some form of focused prayer that allows you to commit yourself to God and God's work in and through you for the day.

- **Are there other elements beyond the four core ingredients you want to include?**

- If you're committing to sessions shorter than 20 minutes, you won't have time for anything beyond the four core elements.

- Any additional elements ought to focus closely on the areas of personal and spiritual growth you're most interested in.

- If you have several other things you want to add, you may want to consider expanding your journaling into a full First Things First (FTF) routine. Review Week 6, Day 3 for what this might look like.

DOING A PERIODIC REVIEW

Your journaling practice can and should evolve, adapting to your season of life and needs. Make minor adaptations to keep your practice sustainable. Doing a periodic review will also ensure that your practice remains relevant, helpful, and on track.

A periodic review gives you a gracious opportunity to discontinue elements that are no longer meaningful, or change the way you're incorporating the four core elements. It allows you to experiment with new components knowing you aren't committed to them forever. I do my review every year in the fall, which is a natural season for setting new goals and expectations. Find a cycle that makes sense for you.

In this review, you have two goals. First, do what you can to remove any obstacles or friction points that make showing up for journaling more difficult. Second, ensure that your current template remains relevant to your needs and sense of God's invitation. You may also want to review the content of your journal over this past season. You may notice themes worth digging into. One reader commented that it was looking back over her journals that helped her identify that she had Seasonal Affective Disorder. So pay attention to the content as well.

When you make changes, keep the **Trigger > Journal > Reward** cycle in mind. (If you need to, go back to Week 5, Day 3, to review this concept.) Don't change so many things that you break your trigger. These questions can guide you through your review:

- **Is your length of time and time of day working?**

  - Are you finding that you regularly go over time? Would expanding your time commitment be useful? Or do you think this upcoming season of life might require you to shorten your journaling commitment in order to maintain it without going into overload? Sustainability is key.

  - Does your current time of day work well for you? Are you able to hold the necessary length of time without distraction or unmanageable pressure from other commitments?

  - Has your life changed enough that committing to a different length or time of day would make journaling easier?

  - If needed, review Week 2, Days 2 & 3 for best practices and issues that impact your selection of length and time.

- **Is your location working?**

  - Is your current location supporting your journaling habit well, or are you finding it distracting? Is there a location that would work better?

  - Has your life changed enough that choosing a new location would make journaling easier?

  - If needed, review Week 2, Day 2 for best practices and issues regarding location.

- **Are your tools working for you?**

  - Is your current mode of journaling (analog or digital) working smoothly for you? If your tools are causing friction (journal not where you expect it, journal app not working well), can you do something to make things easier?

  - If you journal on paper, does your journal have enough pages to make it through the next season? Do you have enough of your preferred pens or pencils?

- If you journal digitally, is your current app or program working for you? Does it work smoothly and get out of the way, or do you have to fiddle with it constantly? Would it make journaling easier if you made a change to something else?
- If needed, review Week 2, Day 4 for best practices and issues regarding the tools you use, as well as recommendations in Appendix 3: Recommended Tools.

- **How is your practice of silence going?**
  - How long can you sit in silence comfortably now? Are you ready to expand the length?
  - Is your mind settling into the silence well? If not, are you using tools like focusing on your breath or the Jesus Prayer?
  - What changes would you like to make to improve your practice of silence?
  - If needed, review Week 3, Day 2 for the purpose of silence and simple ways to implement it. You can also check the resource in Appendix 4, "Ways to Practice Silence," for additional ideas.

- **Does it seem helpful to change your focus for Inward Reflection?**
  - If you included a particular focus for personal and spiritual growth in your template, is that area of focus still relevant?
  - If that area remains relevant, are there changes you'd like to make based on what you've learned and how you've grown?
  - If that area is no longer relevant, do you have a sense of direction for a new area of focus? If you don't, you could make this a matter of reflection for several days, inviting God to guide you toward a new area of growth.
  - If you've been using scripture, a daily devotional, or some other reading as your prompt, is this working for

you? Do you want to make a change in what you use for an external prompt?

- If needed, Review Week 3, Day 3 for the basics of Inward Reflection.

- For other ideas to use for Inward Reflection, see the resources below in Appendix 4, "Using Scripture for Reflection," "Using Other Reading for Reflection," "Recommended Daily Devotionals," and "Options for Inward Reflection."

- **Does it seem helpful to change your current focus or process of Godward Reflection?**

  - If you included a particular focus for Godward reflection, is that area of focus still relevant?

  - If that area remains important, are there changes you'd like to make based on how you've grown?

  - Do you have a sense of direction for a new area of focus? If you don't, you could make this a matter of reflection for several days, inviting God to guide you toward a new area of focus for growth.

  - If you've been using scripture, a daily devotional, or some other reading as your prompt, is this working for you? Do you want to make a change in what you use for an external prompt?

  - If needed, Review Week 3, Day 4 for the basics of Godward Reflection.

  - For other ideas to use for Inward Reflection, see the resources below in Appendix 4, "Using Scripture for Reflection," "Using Other Reading for Reflection," "Recommended Daily Devotionals," and "Options for Inward Reflection."

- **Are there any changes you'd like to make to your prayer practice that ends your journal session?**

  - Is your current prayer practice serving your needs and sense of direction? Is it meaningful?

  - Is there something you should drop or add?

- **If you're including other elements beyond the four core ingredients, are they continuing to serve you?**
  - Are you ready to phase out any current additional elements that are no longer serving you?
  - Are there areas of growth you'd like to address by adding new elements to your journaling template? What area of growth would you like to address? What is a simple reflective process you could add that will help guide you in that direction?
  - Are you ready to expand your time so that you can include additional elements? Are there elements beyond journaling that you want to add, moving in the direction of a full First Things First (FTF) routine? Review Week 6, Day 3 for the basics of what this might look like.
- **Having reviewed your tools and template, articulate the changes you are making for this next season.**
  - In your journal, make a note of any changes you're making and why you're making them. This will give you focus for the new season, and give you a reference when you come to the next periodic review.
  - If you're changing time, location, or the tools you're using, do what's necessary to implement these changes. Get the supplies you need. Make the necessary arrangements.
  - If you're changing your template, write your new template out fresh. If you're journaling on paper, print out a new copy to use as a bookmark and reference, or write it out on a reference page in your journal. If you're journaling digitally, update your template file or make a new one if you want to keep the old one for reference.

RECOMMENDED TOOLS

Note: I provide links to various resources below. These links were accurate and functional at the time of publication. Also, in a few cases, the links are affiliate links, which means that if you purchase that book or product through my link, I'll get an infinitesimal kick-back from the retailer, which I promise to spend on buying more books. When it comes to affiliate links, it is my practice only to recommend books or resources that I have personally used and found helpful.

TOOLS TO AID DIGITAL JOURNALING

Digital journaling has several benefits. If you're a person who keeps your devices close, then your journal is always accessible. A digital journal has infinite pages, can be easily searched when you want to look up something from a past entry, can include links and images, and can be secure. On the other hand, digital journaling happens on the same device with all your other apps, so it can also be a distracting environment.

- **What Device Works Best?**
  - Any computer or tablet with an external keyboard is OK. Unless you're using speech-to-text, small phones or tablets with only touch-screen keyboards will be an obstacle for most people.
  - The best device is the one you're familiar with and have at hand.
  - An interesting possibility: A therapist I trust suggested that journaling on a keyboard has the advantage of stimulating both hemispheres of the brain, like EMDR does in trauma processing or walking and talking does when thinking through a problem. This may provide a neurological advantage to using a computer when writing about emotionally difficult topics.

- **Using a Word Processor**

  - Any word processing software or app works. It's best to use something you're familiar with so you don't have to fiddle with the tool to get it to work for you. Most PCs have **Microsoft Word**. Most Macs have **Pages**. Any computer with a browser can access **Google Docs**. All of these are more than sufficient for journaling.

  - If you use a word processor, don't get distracted by formatting. Create a simple template document for yourself where your sections are pre-formatted. Then copy and paste this template to get started with each new session.

  - A simple plan that works well is to maintain a single journal document rather than making a new document each day. Keep your template at the top of the document. To start a new day, copy and paste that blank template at the top of the document and then do your journaling in the blank template below it. Your most recent entry will always be at the top of the document right after a fresh blank template. You'll build a journal document in reverse chronological order, so it's easy to find past entries. You can start a new document seasonally, annually, or when you update your template.

- **Using a Mobile App**

  - There are many great journaling apps for all the major mobile ecosystems. Pick something that is simple, pleasant to use, and not too fiddly. You want as little friction as possible in your process. One of the benefits of using a mobile app is that these apps usually provide a cloud backup of your journal. This gives you the security that you won't lose your journal entries. If the app is cross-platform, it's even better because you'll be able to access it on whatever device or computer you have available.

  - **Google Docs.** One of the best options that combines low cost (free!), cloud back-up, and cross-platform availability is Google Docs. You can use it in the Chrome browser on any computer, and it has apps available for nearly any tablet or phone. Your journal document will always be backed up and available wherever you are. The downside is that you're storing your data with Google, which almost certainly scans all of your personal information for its own purposes. *www.google.com/ docs/about/*

- **DayOne.** I've used DayOne exclusively for my digital journal for several years. It's only for Mac and iOS and is designed specifically for journaling. It's streamlined, straightforward to use, and provides everything you need, including password protection, multiple journals, the ability to add images and videos, tags, universal search, very simple formatting, cloud back-up, and availability at all your devices. The app is free to use but provides premium features, including cloud storage, for a small fee. *www.dayoneapp.com*

- **Evernote.** A classic note-keeping and journaling app. Evernote is available for Windows, Mac, iOS, and Android operating systems. Evernote is a complete note-keeping system that goes far beyond journaling. You can create a "notebook" for your journal to separate your journal from other notes. Notes can include simple formatting, multimedia, links, voice recordings, and handwriting. Entries are automatically backed up to the cloud. You can try Evernote for free, but all features unlock with a monthly subscription. *www.evernote.com*

- **Managing Notifications & Distraction**

  - If you journal on a computer or mobile device, it is essential that you take steps to manage distractions. It is all too easy to have your focus broken by an email or social media notification or your own inner need to flip over to a work app to quickly handle "one last thing." You will not successfully build a habit of journaling on a device if you can't manage this.

  - **Use your "Do Not Disturb" (DND) function.** Most modern devices have some kind of DND function.

Locate it! This turns off notifications. I cannot overstate how dangerous notification pop-ups are for your journaling process. They will yank your mind right out of your inner world and back into your world of obligation.

- **Turn off your WiFi.** Unless your journaling app requires it, you can further limit the possibility of distraction by turning off your internet access.

- **The Freedom App.** If needed, you can go one step further by using the Freedom App. This tool, available on all modern operating systems and platforms, allows you to turn off your internet and access to certain apps for a specific period. It can work across all your devices simultaneously. It is a lifesaver for me. You can customize what is accessible. I use it to turn off all social media and web browsing while I journal; when writing, I turn off just social media, so I still have browser access for research. It is a flexible tool that will help you focus without distraction. Learn about the app at: *https://bit.ly/3H4sNNG*.

TOOLS TO AID ANALOG JOURNALING

Analog journaling has different benefits. Writing with pen and paper slows you down, which can aid mental focus. It has a classic, even sacred feel for some people. Your paper journal can't run out of batteries. It works whether you have internet or not, and if you accidentally drop your journal on the floor, you won't crack the screen. If you're not worried about your handwriting, value the slower pace of longhand, or want to limit distractions, analog journaling may be the better choice for you.

- **What tools should you use?**

  - Analog journaling means pen and pencil on paper (unless you're really into typing on an old-fashioned type-writer). As you choose your tools, keep them simple and accessible. You want as little friction as possible for your habit.

- **Pen or Pencil?**
  - I prefer pen to pencil because pencil smudges, but pencil can be erased. If you choose pencil, you'll need a sharpener or mechanical pencil lead. If you choose pen, pick one that won't bleed or smear. I recommend:
  - **The Sharpie Pen.** This is *not* the famous marker. It is their excellent thin-barrel, fine-point, fiber-tip pen available in a variety of colors. Great line, saturated ink color, but no bleed-through on most paper and no smearing. This is my go-to pen for every occasion. *https://amzn.to/3DosSzp*
  - **The Pilot G2 Gel Pen.** One of the best pens ever made. It's available in several tip sizes, colors, and barrel styles. A lot of people prefer gel pens because they write so very smoothly. *https://amzn.to/3qlnp2z*
- **What kind of journal?**
  - Your options are limitless. Bound, spiral-bound to lie flat, hand-made, nearly any kind of theme or artwork you like. The only pitfalls to watch out for are running out of pages or being intimidated by a lovely journal you don't want to foul up with messy handwriting.
  - **The Classic Moleskine.** The most famous and iconic bound journal. Available with blank, lined, or dotted pages, in many colors, not least of which is black. They are pricey but will last forever and feel great to write in. *https://amzn.to/3mZ4icU*
  - **The Moleskine Cahier.** When a more expensive hard-bound journal feels too imposing, I love Moleskine's Cahier line, paper-back notebooks with heavy-duty kraft paper covers available in multiple sizes. They travel well. Because of their smaller page count, you more frequently get that fun feeling of "finishing" a journal. *https://amzn.to/3qzpdWb*
  - **Handmade and Unique.** You can find an unending variety of handmade journals with unique covers and styles on *www.Etsy.com*.

WAYS TO PRACTICE

Note: *I provide links to various resources below. These links were accurate and functional at the time of publication. Also, in a few cases, the links are affiliate links, which means that if you purchase that book or product through my link, I'll get an infinitesimal kick-back from the retailer, which I promise to spend on buying more books. When it comes to affiliate links, it is my practice only to recommend books or resources that I have personally used and found helpful.*

WAYS TO PRACTICE SILENCE

Breath Prayers

Breath prayers are an excellent tool to still the mind and body as you enter into a period of silence.

The premise of a breath prayer is simple. It is a prayer short enough to pray in the time it takes to breathe in and out. Often it is broken into two phrases, the inhale and the exhale. The body participates in the prayer by slowly breathing in and out. The mind engages by forming the words silently in thought. In this way, the whole self is focused and can come to rest.

Breath prayers are helpful for several reasons. They are easily memorized. Once they've become associated with your breath through repetition, they can arise spontaneously during the day, providing a way to "pray without ceasing."* Because Breath Prayers tie together body, mind, and spirit, they are also useful to quiet the mind, still the body, and regulate anxiety.

The most famous Christian breath prayer is the Jesus Prayer, an ancient Eastern Orthodox prayer that probably originated with the desert mystics in the 5th century. ***"Lord Jesus Christ, Son of God / Have mercy on me, a sinner."*** But there are so

---

* The Apostle Paul gave this instruction in 1st Thessalonians 5:17. He doesn't elaborate on what he means exactly. Since it's not possible for us to verbally pray without ever stopping, he must have been referring to some kind of contemplative practice.

many other phrases drawn from scripture that work as well. Here are a few:

- *"The Lord is my shepherd / I shall not want."*
- *"I believe / Help my unbelief."*
- *"Lord, make haste to help me. / Lord, make speed to save me."*
- *"Lord, have mercy."*

I teach a longer prayer, called the **Anchor Prayer,** that can be prayed as a breath prayer over two sets of inhaling and exhaling.

(Inhale) *"I rest in faith trusting Father"*
(Exhale) *"I walk in faith following Jesus."*
(Inhale) *"I hear in faith obeying Spirit"*
(Exhale) *"In You, I remain"*

Author Sarah Bessey gives an excellent introduction to breath prayers, how to use them, and several examples in this article: *http://live210.com/bessey-breath/*

A Grounding Body Scan

Part of learning to be in silence is learning to listen carefully to your body. A body scan is a practice that can teach you to settle yourself and notice your body more closely. Follow these steps:

- **Sit in a comfortable chair with your feet flat on the floor and your hands resting on your thighs.**
- **Close your eyes and breathe slowly in and out, counting each breath. Do this until you get to ten.**
- **In your mind's eye, see your body sitting precisely as you are now.**
- **Starting at the crown of your head, slowly take notice of each part of your body.**
  - **Focus on one part of your body in your mental image, and turn your full sensory attention there.**

- Notice whether that part is cold, hot, tense or relaxed. Notice if there is any pain, ache, or other discomforts.

  - Whatever the state of that part of your body, don't do anything; just notice how it feels.

- **When you've taken a moment to feel that part of your body, move to the next part, breathing slowly.**

- **Slowly, over several minutes, check in with each part. Crown, forehead, eyes, ears, nose, mouth, jaw, throat, shoulders, etc., continuing down until you get to the soles of your feet.**

- **When you've finished, keep your eyes closed and breathe slowly in and out ten more times, intentionally relaxing your body.**

Recommended Reading on Silence

Here are books I recommend that address silence:

- **New Seeds of Contemplation** by Thomas Merton. https://amzn.to/3wUyEQW

- **The Way of the Heart: Connecting with God Through Prayer, Wisdom, and Silence** by Henri Nouwen. https://amzn.to/3oDm1hu

- **Silence In the Age of Noise** by Erling Kagge. https://amzn.to/3oGiI9l

- **Befriending Silence: Discovering the Gifts of Cistercian Spirituality**[*] by Carl McColman. https://amzn.to/3oxTAJM

- **A Taste of Silence: Centering Prayer & the Contemplative Journey** by Carl Arico. https://amzn.to/3FuwFpJ

---

[*] The Cistercians are a monastic order that was founded in 1098, and whose order (structure for living a spiritual life) was foundational for many monastic groups that came after them. In the Christian tradition, it has been thoughtful monastics who have spent the most time reflecting on the importance of silence.

- **Celebration of the Disciplines** by Richard Foster. This classic is a treasure that can introduce you to many spiritual practices that have been part of the Christian faith for centuries. https://amzn.to/3FnkhHS

USING SCRIPTURE FOR REFLECTION

Lectio Divina

Lectio Divina (Latin for Divine Reading) is a form of meditation based on scripture. This practice has been found in ancient Christian writing as far back as the 3rd century. Instead of coming to scripture with the intention of studying or understanding doctrine, this practice sees scripture as the location for an encounter with God.

There are many great resources that can teach you this form of reflection. It's made up of four simple phases:

- **Lectio (Reading)** - Read a short passage of scripture. Read it slowly. Read it several times. Read it so that you get past your initial focus on details or theology, letting the words themselves settle into you.

- **Meditatio (Meditation)** - Reread the passage slowly, waiting for the Spirit to draw your attention to something. Don't assign a predetermined meaning to the passage, especially with well-known passages where you're already familiar with the interpretation. Instead, ponder the scene and experience of those within the scene. Enter into the scripture in your mind.

- **Oratio (Prayer)** - Pray the passage back to God, pray on the theme of the passage, or in any other ways you are led to pray.

- **Contemplatio (Contemplation)** - End your time in total silence, being present to God who spoke through scripture and in prayer. If necessary, hold some image in mind from the text to help keep focus.

Starter Scriptures for Reflection

If you want to use scripture as your focus and you're not sure where to start, here's a list you can use. If you journal five days a week, this list will carry you through six weeks.

1. Psalm 19:7-11
2. Psalm 1:1-3
3. Jeremiah 17:7-8
4. John 15:5-8
5. Isaiah 40:31
6. Psalm 139:13-14
7. John 16:33
8. Matthew 6:25
9. Proverbs 3:3-4
10. Isaiah 54:10
11. Galatians 5:1
12. John 15:5
13. 2 Corinthians 4:16
14. Galatians 5:22-23
15. Proverbs 3:3-6
16. Psalm 23
17. Ephesians 2:10
18. Galatians 5:13
19. Isaiah 49:15-16
20. Colossians 3:12
21. Psalms 130:1-2
22. Romans 8:1-2
23. Isaiah 30:18
24. 2nd Corinthians 12:9
25. Matthew 11:28
26. Ephesians 1:18
27. James 1:17
28. 1st Corinthians 13:4-5
29. 1st John 4:12
30. Psalms 51:1-2

Using a Lectionary

Historically, most churches have used a lectionary to guide their scripture reading. This tool presents scripture week by week. Most commonly used for weekly worship, it is a fantastic guide for personal scripture reading and meditation.

- **The Revised Common Lectionary.** The most widely used lectionary is the Revised Common Lectionary (RCL) of the Anglican Church. Each week of the year, it presents one reading from Psalms, one from the Hebrew Scriptures,* one from the Gospels, and one from the rest of the New Testament. Over three years, the RCL touches on the entire scope of scripture. The RCL can be bought in book form, but it is also available online in various places for free, like this easy to use site: *https://lectionary.library.vanderbilt.edu*

- **A Woman's Lectionary for the Whole Church.** Hebrew scholar and Womanist theologian Dr. Wilda Gafney has compiled a lectionary that brings the women of scripture into focus. This brings needed balance by drawing attention to God's work in and through women. She has a version that covers the gospels in one year (Called "Year W," *https://amzn.to/3wVcQVg*) and has released the first part of a three-year cycle that will touch on the whole scope of scripture (Called "Year A," *https://amzn.to/3Cl6qzW*).

- The Jewish faith uses a similar weekly reading schedule of the Torah (The books of Genesis, Exodus, Leviticus, Numbers and Deuteronomy). This weekly scripture is called **the Torah portion,** *parsha,* or *parashah.* This practice is quite ancient, possibly going back to the time of the Babylonian exile in the 6th century BCE. It is quite likely that the Christian tradition of lectionary use was an adaptation of this much older practice. A very accessible presentation of the weekly parsha can be found here: *https://www.alephbeta.org/weekly-torah-portion.*

---

*The first part of the Bible that Christians often call the Old Testament. I prefer to identify this as the Hebrew Scriptures both to acknowledge that it is the portion of the Bible written in Hebrew and, more importantly, to identify that it is originally and continues to be the scriptures of the Jewish faith.

Using Other Readings for Reflection

Other readings outside of scripture can be used profitably as prompts for our inward and Godward reflection. What kind of reading works? Almost anything, if you keep the following principles in mind.

- **Readings need to be short.** How short? One page at most. If it's already formatted that way, great. If it's not, it needs to be the kind of writing that can be taken in short chunks.

- **Choose depth.** Choose books by authors who not only have a spiritual intention but have real-life experience to bring to the table. Choose old books that have stood the test of time. Choose deep books rather than popular ones.

- **Be careful with devotionals.** Because writing short chunks seems easy, a lot of people write devotional books. Most of them are superficial and trite. Writing something that is both short and deep is the most challenging kind of writing. Just because a devotional is famous or popular doesn't mean it's rich and deep. The best review of a devotional book is when someone you consider spiritually mature tells you that a devotional was meaningful to them.

No matter what you choose, remember that you're going to be considering each reading from two vantages, **Inward Reflection** and **Godward Reflection**. First, you'll read the selection and then reflect on it in light of your own inner life. Come to the passage with questions like these:

1. **How does this reading reflect on my inner life?**

2. **What does it say about who I am and who I want to be?**

3. **How does this reading touch on my thoughts, feelings, beliefs, and motivations?**

4. **How does this reading reflect on my relationships?**

Second, using the same selection, allow it to speak to you about who God is, what God is like, and how this view of God impacts you. Come to the selection with questions like these:

1. **What does this reading suggest about God's character?**

2. **If God is like this, what does it mean for me? For the world?**

3. **Have I seen or experienced God working in this way in my life?**

4. **Does this reading invite me to any kind of response?**

Recommended Daily Devotionals

Thousands of daily devotional books have been written. Below I recommend some time-tested classics as well as a few that have moved me deeply.

- **The Listening Day: Meditations on the Way.** This is a beautifully written 2-volume set by Paul J. Pastor. This is probably my favorite all-time daily devotional and rich enough to reward multiple readings. *https://amzn.to/3HyzPuo*

- **Spiritual Classics.** This is a selection of classic Christian contemplative writing spanning two millennia, organized in 52 short readings with brief commentary by Richard Foster. If you aren't familiar with the riches of historic Christian spirituality, this is a great sampler for you. *https://amzn.to/3Hx1E65*

- **You Are Enough: Learning to Love Yourself the Way God Loves You.** This devotional by Jonathan Puddle is the first I've come across that is trauma-informed. While written from a Christian perspective, it's written broadly enough to be meaningful to people from any faith background. I highly recommend it. *https://amzn.to/3noM3gW*

- Jonathan Puddle offers another devotional I highly recommend. **Mornings With God: Daily Bible Devotional For Men.** Jonathan wrote this at the request of a publisher, and it's quite unique. The daily entries are very short—perfect for including in a 15 or 30 minute journaling routine, but Jonathan builds a beautiful narrative over the 365 entries. The "for men" part is very light and comes from a non-patriarchal viewpoint, so I recommend this for anyone. *https://amzn.to/3dkOZZw*

- **My Utmost for His Highest,** by Oswald Chambers, is one of the most widely read classic daily devotionals. *https://amzn.to/3CtrPa2*

- **Streams in the Desert.** This is a 365-day devotional by Lettie Cowman. Another long-standing classic from 1925 written by a woman missionary. *https://amzn.to/30CfymZ*

Other Recommended Spiritual Reading

You can use other spiritual books as your prompt even if they aren't written in a daily devotional format. Just make sure to read only a short segment, one page or less, so you can focus your reflection.

- **The Imitation of Christ.** Almost six hundred years old, this book continues to move people, by Thomas a Kempis. *https://amzn.to/3CtsjwS*

- **The Interior Castle.** Written in 1580 by Teresa of Avila, this is one of the classics of Christian contemplative literature. *https://amzn.to/3Dt3Hpy*

- **Practicing the Presence of God.** A simple little book by Brother Lawrence, written in 1692. *https://amzn.to/3wWIXDY*

- **A Testament of Devotion** by Thomas Kelly, a Quaker pastor. *https://amzn.to/3oxhPaQ*

- **Life Together** by Dietrich Bonhoeffer, a Lutheran pastor who wrote this in secret during Nazi persecution. A brief and practical guide to spiritual growth and life in community. *https://amzn.to/3Csl5cP*

- **Return of the Prodigal** by Henri Nouwen. Meditations on Jesus' most famous story. *https://amzn.to/30DIx1F*

- **The Ragamuffin Gospel** by Brennan Manning. Jesus' message for those on the bottom of society, religion, and in their own view of themselves. *https://amzn.to/3qNOaNC*

- **Woman to Woman: An Anthology of Women's Spiritualities.** This is a collection of writing from 15 different spiritual women spanning a thousand years. *https://amzn.to/30B2Ggn*

- **New Seeds of Contemplation** by Thomas Merton. *https://amzn.to/3Cr54Um*

- **Space for God: Study and Practice of Spirituality and Prayer** by Don Postema. *https://amzn.to/3kMkKeG*

- **Present Perfect** by Greg Boyd. This little volume is the best introduction to contemplative living I've ever come across. It's simple, clear, practical, and can help you change the way you see your life. *https://amzn.to/3qMCgTX*

- **Sacred Pathways** by Gary Thomas. This book talks about how different spiritual practices are fruitful for different personality types. *https://amzn.to/3kJbybi*

Using Poetry as a Spiritual Focus

Because of the necessary economy of words, poetry can often create a lot of space for reflection. It's potent when the poet is also someone with a spiritual and contemplative focus in their lives. Some great options:

- **Emily Dickinson** (1830-1886), American poet. *Hope is the Thing With Feathers: The Complete Poems of Emily Dickinson* is an excellent source. *https://amzn.to/3FnujZF*

- **Mary Oliver** (1935-2019) American poet. I recommend *Devotions: The Selected Poems of Mary Oliver.* *https://amzn.to/30Civ73*

- **Pádraig Ó Tuama** (Living) Irish poet and theologian. *Readings from the Book of Exile* is a good place to start. *https://amzn.to/3HH1MQO*

- **Rumi** (1207-1273) Iranian Sufi poet. *The Sufi Path of Love* is a good translation with poems arranged by theme and some short commentary. *https://amzn.to/3HuboOB*

- **Rainer Rilke** (1875-1926) Austrian author and poet. *The Book of Hours* particularly focuses on prayer and the search for God. *https://amzn.to/3FnurbB*

- **Hafez Shiraz** (1315-1390) Persian poet and Sufi mystic. Be mindful when you look for Hafez. There is an English-speaking poet named Daniel Ladinsky who offers his original poetry as "translations" of Hafez. Many of the Hafez quotes you see around the internet come from him rather than any historical source. *The Faces of Love* is an excellent modern english translation of authentic Hafez poetry. *https://amzn.to/3CqMls3*

- **John Donne** (1572-1631) English poet. Try *John Donne: Selections from Divine Poems, Sermons, Devotions and Prayers*. *https://amzn.to/3FGSX7R*

- **Elizabeth Barrett Browning** (1806-1861) English poet. *Browning: Poems* includes poetry by Elizabeth as well as by her husband, Robert Browning. *https://amzn.to/3oIcy8x*

- **The Soul in Paraphrase** is a collection of devotional poetry from across the centuries. This makes it an easy starting point for using poetry as a spiritual focus. *https://amzn.to/3CqHh78*

ADDITIONAL OPTIONS FOR INWARD REFLECTION

There are many ways to focus inward reflection. This is where you think about who you are, who you are becoming, and what life teaches you. A few suggestions:

- **The Ignatian Examen.** This is a form of reflective prayer designed by Ignatius of Loyola in 1522. There are many resources on how to use it, but here it is in simple terms:

    1. **Be quiet and pray your intention to receive God's insight on the state of your soul.**

    2. **Pray gratitude for anything in the previous day you are thankful for.**

    3. **Review the last day. Ask the Spirit to give you clarity as you think through the events and interactions of the previous day.** What do you notice? What stands out? What emotions did you feel and why? Did God seem near or distant?

    4. **Respond. Present to God whatever comes up as you reflect on your day.** Ask for forgiveness, restoration, and healing for moments that were destructive. Ask for the next steps you ought to take. Pray gratitude for moments of grace.

    5. **Look Forward. Pray through your expectations for the next day, inviting God to guide you.** You could use the Lord's Prayer as a model for praying through your coming day.

    6. **Silent Reflection.** End with silent listening.

- **Reflecting On Your Goals.** Bringing your life goals and plans before God is a beneficial form of inward reflection. Your journal can be a place where you record those goals and reflect on them, asking God's guidance. This also can become a natural way to track how you are doing with those goals. This doesn't need to be a daily part of your process, but you could come back to it periodically—

quarterly or once a year—and give a bit more time to talking your goals through with God.

- **A Log of Emotions.** For people who struggle with feeling or knowing what their emotions mean, keeping track of emotions can be a helpful way to grow in this area. This can be as detailed as a running emotional log noting whenever a significant emotional change comes over you and why. It can also just be a segment in your journaling where, for a few minutes, you reflect on your emotional state since you last journaled. This will help you begin to see patterns, notice how your body responds to emotion, and learn to identify your emotions more quickly.

- **Dreams.** Some people have vivid dreams. Because your dreams are one of the ways your mind unpacks and sorts your life experiences, dreams can contain helpful insight about your inner life. The Bible even suggests this is one of the ways God communicates with us. Some people have found that writing a brief narrative of their dreams in their journal helps them notice patterns and insights there.

  - **Important Note:** Dream Interpretation is a bucket of worms that has always intrigued humanity. It's something well-trained therapists sometimes do, and a lot of crack-pots! Dreams can be meaningful without having to delve into the murk of dream interpretation.

    - **Here are some simple things to consider if you're wondering about any wisdom your dreams may offer:**

    - **Note the emotions.** If you feel a particular emotion strongly in a dream, consider where that emotion is occurring in your waking life. Strong emotion can often tie the dream experience to waking experience and help you make sense of it.

    - **Notice Repetition.** If you have the same dream repeatedly, or the same kind of theme appears over and over in subsequent dreams, take note of that theme. Very often, this theme will also have importance in your waking life.

- **All the characters in your dream are likely you.** If you dream of interacting with other people or seeing other people, it may help to wonder if those people represent some part of yourself. For example, if someone in your dream is doing something that annoys you, it may be worth considering if you do something similar.

- **Focus on the Questions Raised.** Instead of looking for a specific interpretation, focus on any questions the dream raises. i.e., "Why was I so worried about losing my house in that dream?" Or "Why was I so angry at the person who gave me the gift?" Those questions may point you to useful wisdom for your waking life.

- **The Miracle Question.** This insightful question comes from Solutions-focused Therapy, but I've found it incredibly helpful for discerning steps you need to take, particularly when facing as obstacle or complex problem. This question is often used with depression, anxiety, relational struggles, or other intractable difficulties, but it can provide insight into nearly any obstacle we're facing.

  - Here's the question: *"Imagine that tonight while you sleep, a miracle occurs which completely resolves your problem. When you awake, what would be different in your life? What are some of the things you'd notice that would tell you that this problem no longer existed?"*

  - Free-write your response to this question in your journal, imagining as many details as you can that might clue you in that the problem no longer exists.

  - When that's complete, reflect on your response. Are there things you came up with that you can move toward now, even while the problem exists? If you can't move toward these things, consider why that is? What motivations or inner conflicts are making this problem worse?

ADDITIONAL OPTIONS FOR GODWARD REFLECTION

There are many ways to focus Godward in your reflection. This is when you reflect on God's character, nature, and the ways God seems to have been active in your life, your tradition, or the world. What we think about God will always shape the way we see ourselves and the world around us. If you're using a journal template that includes a prompt from scripture, a daily devotional, or another book, that prompt will be your starting point for thinking about God's character and presence in your life. Beyond that prompt, there are additional ways to incorporate Godward reflection in your journaling time:

- **Scripture Study.** While I said earlier that study of scripture and journaling are two different practices, for some people, including a block of scripture study into the journaling template or FTF practice can be fruitful. Of course, this requires having the necessary resources at hand and a minimum of 30 extra minutes for your journaling time, but it can be rich and meaningful.

- In your journal, note the passage you're studying. Then as you study, record your observations and insights. Note the questions that come up for you. Record notes from your study materials. Note where there are points of connection between the scripture and your life. Here are a few books I've found that are helpful:

  - **How to Read the Bible for All Its Worth,** Gordon Fee. This is the best primer on how to read and study scripture I've ever come across. I consider it mandatory reading for anyone wanting to read the Bible intelligently. *https://amzn.to/3Fqy9kJ*

  - **The Bible Tells Me So: Why Defending Scripture Has Made Us Unable To Read It.** Pete Enns. *https://amzn.to/3HyDjgs*

  - **Reading While Black: African American Biblical Interpretation as an Exercise in Hope.** Esau McCaulley. *https://amzn.to/3kLBSl5*

- **Eat This Book: A Conversation on the Art of Spiritual Reading.** Eugene Peterson. *https://amzn.to/3DsFsYy*

- **Womanist Midrash: A Reintroduction to the Women of the Torah and the Throne.** Dr. Wilda Gafney. *https://amzn.to/3Hxp8rR*

- **The Last Word: Scripture and the Authority of God —Getting Beyond the Bible Wars.** N.T. Wright *https://amzn.to/3nqSP64*

- **Worship.** Some people find that including a time of worship is helpful for feeling connected to God. In this sense, the word worship refers to activities that are explicitly focused on Godward adoration. Listen to some worship songs, or sing yourself. Do something creative like writing poetry or personalizing a Psalm. Pray as you feel led. Worship for whatever time you give yourself. When you return to your journal, note any insights or sense of connection you had with God during worship. This can be a great way to start your journaling time.

Appendix 5
Literature on Habit Building

Notable studies

- **Making health habitual: The Psychology of Habit Formation and General Practices.** Peer-reviewed article with a great list of references for further study. *https://www.ncbi.nlm.nih.gov/pmc/articles/PMC3505409/*

- **How are habits formed: Modeling habit formation in the real world.** Academic research on the formation of habits. Key findings include that missing a single day does not seriously impair habit formation, and that habit formation can take quite a bit longer than expected. *https://onlinelibrary.wiley.com/doi/abs/10.1002/ejsp.674*

Insightful books

- **Atomic Habits: An Easy and Proven Way to Build Good Habits & Break Bad Ones,** by James Clear. *https://amzn.to/3ooFaNG*

- **Change or Die: The Three Keys to Change at Work and in Life,** by Alan Deutchsman. This book is on my top list of recommendations for people who work with people in any role that focuses on life change. *https://amzn.to/3mjuX2n*

- **Elastic Habits: How to Create Smarter Habits that Adapt to Your Day,** by Stephen Guise. *https://amzn.to/3QUzvty*

- **Tiny Habits: The Small Changes that Change Everything,** by B.J. Fogg, PhD. *https://amzn.to/3PEPACI*

- **The Power of Habit: Why We Do What We Do In Life and Business,** by Charles Duhigg. *https://amzn.to/3dMjcAK*

THANK YOU SO MUCH!

Thank you so much for reading this book. I am continually amazed that in a world of nearly infinite information, someone would take their valuable time and read words I've written. I'm humbled when those words turn out to be helpful.

The process I've shared with you here has been invaluable to me, and I've seen it serve others equally well over the years. It's my honor to share with you the lessons I've learned. I hope that all of this serves you well in your pursuit of spiritual maturity.

If you've found this helpful, I'd love to hear your story. Everything I write and do online can be found by going to my website **www.MarcAlanSchelske.com**. I write about practical spiritual growth in the realm that lies beyond the constricting influence of fundamentalism. You can find me on social media: Twitter (@Schelske), Facebook (@MarcAlanSchelske), and also over on Instagram (@MarcAlanSchelske) or you can email me at Marc@MarcAlanSchelske.com. If you take the time to email, and you're not a jerk, I'll respond.

Remember, in this one present moment, you are loved, you are known, and you are not alone.

Other Things from Marc

The Wisdom Of Your Heart

Are you listening to the wisdom of your heart? Your emotions are trying to tell you something. Learning to listen to the truth revealed in our emotions is not only important for a well-lived life but also vital for spiritual growth. Available wherever books are sold. Available in paperback, ebook, and audiobook read by the author.

https://marcalanschelske.com/the-wisdom-of-your-heart/

Untangle Workbook

Emotions don't have to be confusing. They are messages from our deepest places, and they bring with them important understanding—if we can learn how to listen. When we learn this skill, our emotions can become a resource for wisdom to help us navigate life and relationships well. Lay-flat ring-bound journal with prompts for systematically processing emotional experiences. Available on Amazon and at Marc's website:

https://marcalanschelske.com/untangled-workbook/

The Untangled Heart Workshop

Trauma therapist Byron Kehler, M.S., and Marc Alan Schelske present this 5-hour online training that addresses the role emotions play in a healthy life, what is happening in the brain and body when we feel emotions, and a simple-to-understand roadmap for experiencing and understanding those emotions.

https://live210.com/untangle-online/

Discover Your Authentic Core Values

Other people's agendas are competing for your time and resources. You use a schedule and a budget so that your time and money are used intentionally. Without those tools, your decisions would be pulled in every direction by other people's wants and needs. Identifying your core values will help you stop living in reactivity. *Discovering Your Authentic Core Values* walks you step-by-step through a simple process that will help you name what is truly most important to you. Available on Amazon and at Marc's website:

https://marcalanschelske.com/core-values-book/

Not Just One More Thing: Spiritual Growth For Busy People

Is it possible to grow spiritually in the midst of a busy life? You want to grow, but your life is full and fast-paced. You want to slow down, but you're not sure how. Making ends meet, raising kids, moving forward in your career—these things all take time and energy, and you can't opt out of most of them. This ten-week online course can help you find a way forward toward a life that is more than just keeping your spiritual head above water. The course is designed to fit into an already busy life, and it will help you make tangible changes quickly.

https://live210.com/busy-growth/

CPSIA information can be obtained
at www.ICGtesting.com
Printed in the USA
JSHW071416251122
33763JS00002B/12